The Lampmaking Handbook

Photo Credits

Cover: **A. Kravitz**
Back Cover: **A. Kravitz**

Tiffany Style Lamps By Joe Porcelli

Geometric Lamp: **Jim Mercer**
Bouquet Lamp: **Michael D'Orio**
Tulip on Bronze Urn Base: **A. Kravitz**

Original Lamps By Joe Porcelli

Landscape Through Large Windows: **Michael D'Orio**
Murnau 1909: **Michael D'Orio**
Sails On Red: **Michael D'Orio**

Book and Cover Design: **Christopher Peterson**

The Lampmaking Handbook

First American Edition

Copyright © 1991 by Joseph Porcelli

ISBN 0-9629053-6-4

Library of Congress catalog card no. 91-70829

Published by
The Glass Press
PO Box 678
Richboro, PA 18954
(215) 579-2720

Printed and Manufactured in the United States of America

Cover: *20" Bouquet Lamp*, 1985, J. Porcelli

Frontispiece: *18" Rose Border Lamp*, 1990, J. Porcelli

Acknowledgments

Many people contributed to the creation of this book. Some may not realize it, but they have. Nonetheless, I am indebted to them for their help, advice, direction, criticism, and most of all, their patience.

I would like to thank Chris Peterson for his editorial endurance, Monona Rossol for her excellent contributions concerning health and safety, and my family, to whom this book must have seemed a never-ending quest over the three years it took to get it to press.

Also I would like to thank the following: Albert Lewis, Joanne Nervo, Jack Sciarabba, Chris Thornton, Stan Schlesinger, Jim Hicks, Jenny French, Paul Crist, Jim Schlitz, Greg Williams, Paul Stankard, Michael D'Orio, Chris and Vicki Payne, Youghiogheny Glass, Bullseye Glass Co., Uroboros Glass Co., Alan Kravitz, and the lampmakers and students who, I hope, will profit from this effort.

Contents

1

A Useful Overview

Time spent learning about or how to do new things enriches our lives and makes them more interesting. In the world of artistic creation, time nurtures our knowledge and experience. The personal projects and endeavors to which we devote the most time are usually the ones that reap the greatest rewards.

Learning to make a stained, or "leaded" glass lamp requires, more than anything else, an investment of time. Here, as in any craft, the time spent on practice, and the quality of that time, will be translated into your accomplishments.

The Lampmaking Tradition

The name Tiffany reigns supreme in any discussion of the stained glass lamp. Although his studio did not invent it, no company was more instrumental in establishing and promoting the stained glass lamp as a member of the American decorative arts. The development of the stained glass lamp was guided by Tiffany's aesthetic and technical advances from the late 19th century well into the 20th. Other firms made lamps, but none to the extent and popularity of the Tiffany Studios.

Louis Comfort Tiffany's extraordinary vision and considerable resources enabled him and his company to explore and invent new ways of presenting this art form to an eager and affluent public. His methods, techniques and innovations were copied, some rather successfully, but never equalled in scope or quality. It is upon the Tiffany tradition that fine stained glass lampmaking has developed. Today, we look upon the creations of Tiffany's craftspeople with a certain amount of awe, drawing from them an endless source of inspiration.

At one time, I wanted nothing more than to be able to achieve in my work the kind of beauty and excellence the lamps of the Tiffany Studios displayed. My working experience afforded me the opportunity to puzzle together the processes and techniques necessary to lampmaking. I can now share that knowledge with you.

The Project At Hand

This book describes two lampmaking projects. The first is the preparation and processes required to build a Tiffany-style, 18" Rose Border lamp. The second is geared to the more adventurous or experienced artisan and deals with developing a design on a blank lamp mold, or form. In this section, the steps taken to bring the 18" Rose Border lamp design from conception to construction will be outlined.

A number of products are available to assist you in building a leaded glass lamp. Many of the most popular Tiffany designs, from the smallest and simplest geometric lamps to the legendary Wisteria, are available in both kit and design form. Other non-Tiffany, period styles can be had as well. These vary in size from 12" to 28" in diameter and from under 400 pieces of glass to almost 2,000. For my instructions and illustrations, I have chosen a lamp that is neither so simple, nor so complex, as to give a distorted presentation of the craft and its attendant techniques. Although it is not a Tiffany design per se, it is based entirely on the Tiffany style and methods of design and fabrication. The tools, materials and design aids used are all available to craftspeople through stained glass retail establishments and art supply stores.

I have also outlined the preparation of an original design on a blank lamp form. Should you ever consider building a lamp using your own artwork, the availability of this information will equip you and your craftspeople to that specific end. Once you have mastered building a lamp from existing design aids, the next natural step is an original work.

How To Use This Book
This book can be used in two different ways. It can be read from front to back as a complete course in lampmaking, or it can be used as a reference guide. If you are new to lampmaking, I would suggest you follow the instructions in the book as they are written, in a logical, step-by-step fashion. Each chapter can also stand alone as a complete informational unit. Should you wish to know more about glass cutting, for instance, you can turn to that specific chapter for an in-depth discussion of the topic.

The safety information included is very important. All too often, safety is overlooked when practicing stained glass, and other crafts as well. Whether pursuing an enjoyable pastime or attempting to make a living with your lampmaking, there is no need to compromise your, or anyone else's personal safety for the art. Several of the materials and practices used in making a stained glass lamp are considered potentially hazardous. These dangers can be avoided through an awareness of the hazards involved and taking some basic precautions. Safety in craft doesn't require a great effort.

Monona Rossol has written the safety chapter, chapter 11, for this book. She has written for Professional Stained Glass magazine and is the President of Arts Crafts and Theater Safety (ACTS) in New York City. She is a highly regarded professional and an extremely knowledgeable industrial hygienist. I insist you read this chapter, as the information Ms. Rossol provides will identify those areas of the craft where safety should be an underlying and ongoing concern. Conscientious work habits governing the proper use of materials and a concern for the working environment will add to the pleasure of the craft of lampmaking and help assure a safe, comfortable work place. Establish safe working habits early and they will become a natural part of your work ■

2

Getting Started

Lampmaking is comprised of a number of integrated techniques, each requiring a certain amount of attention and time to complete. For the purposes of this book, I have chosen a relatively simple lamp design, one that will provide a clear and easy display of the many aspects and techniques related to building a leaded glass lamp. Getting involved with a very large lamp (i.e., a Wisteria) is certainly a challenge, but is not generally a wise decision for the beginner.

You are learning a new craft. Your immediate goal should be to familiarize yourself with new techniques, applying them to a project that will allow you to concentrate on learning the skill without getting yourself bogged down with an enormous workload. Having to cut and wrap 1,000 pieces of glass before you get into the actual creation of the lamp can prove counterproductive and frustrating.

Start small and build your knowledge and capabilities with each successive project. If you pursue lampmaking as a hobby, you will gain great satisfaction from your efforts and realize progress from lamp to lamp. As a professional, seeking to add to your artistic offerings, you will want your lamps to reflect the professional quality your clients expect. Don't compromise your success with a hasty choice or overwhelming work load. Above all else, your lampmaking experience should be a rewarding and fulfilling one.

Lamps come in many shapes, sizes and styles; lamp designs present a veritable world of considerations. Representational landscapes depicting flowers, landscapes, decorative patterns, etc., are abundant. Designs created by the Tiffany Studios are the most popular, with turn-of-the-century Victorian, Art Nouveau, and Art Deco designs readily available, as well. Abstract or contemporary lamp designs, although gaining in popularity, are not readily available in kit form. Designing and building such lamps will be fully discussed in chapter 9, "Designing Your Own Lamp."

The size of your chosen lamp (the diameter of the shade) should be kept within a reasonable limit for your first project. A 14", 16" or 18" shade is easier to handle, from a physical standpoint, than a larger shade. The combination of glass and solder on a lamp mold increases the manageable weight of the project appreciably. A 22" shade can easily approach 15 pounds in accrued material weight. It is no mean task to juggle that weight around for hours at a time during lamp construction. It is best to start with a shade that will be manageable.

Shades ranging from 12" to 20" diameter are the commonly used for table lamps and can easily be matched with a suitable base. Where interior design allows, smaller shades can be hung from the ceiling.

Traditional, representational lamp design is easily broken down into integrated elements. Each design can be considered in terms of foreground, background and borders. Foreground is composed of identifiable objects, such as flowers, leaves and stems; background is the surrounding blank area (containing no image elements), and borders are frame-like peripheral glass pieces usually set in a simple and pleasing geometric pattern.

Lamp designs can consist of background without foreground, as in monochromatic (one color) geometric patterns, foreground with little background, where the design is so much of the shade's surface that background pieces are hardly visible, and compositions made of both geometric and naturalistic elements, such as the one demonstrated in this text.

Any of these design combinations will work as a first project. Remember, the number of glass pieces in relation to the complexity and size of the lamp determine the work load. The 18" Rose lamp we will construct contains 366 pieces of glass. Its design incorporates a geometric grid around the dome, or upper half of the shade, and features a naturalistic depiction of roses and leaves around its skirt or lower half. The design repeats three times.

A geometric, monochromatic design is also a suitable beginning project, although geometric shades are not necessarily the easiest to execute, because cutting and assembling the glass requires a good deal of accuracy. The repetitive nature of the glass pieces, however, and the lack of complicated color considerations may free a craftsperson to concentrate entirely on con-

struction technique while leaving the aesthetics for a later project. The drawback to working on a geometric design is exactly that which makes it attractive—repetitiveness. Your choice should be a practical one, but you must also choose a design that pleases you and that will maintain your interest in the craft.

There are many Tiffany lamp designs available that incorporate a reasonable number of glass pieces (less than 500) and can be considered for beginning projects. Here are a few with the number of glass pieces in each. All are commercially available:

14"* Daffodil Cone .... 387 Pieces
16" Vine Ornament .... 432 Pieces
16" Apple Blossom .... 338 Pieces
16" Poppy .... 381 Pieces
16" Acorn .... 468 Pieces
16" Woodbine .... 225 Pieces
18" Peony .... 513 Pieces
20" Waterlily .... 420 Pieces

*Inches indicate diameter of shade.

Most lamp designs "repeat" around a shade's surface. Think of a lamp's surface as being sectioned into three, four, six, or even nine equal parts with the sectional border lines radiating from the very top (or apex) to the bottom border, and a perfect copy of the design repeating in each of these sections. This effective way of filling the lamp's surface has become standard practice and serves the medium well in a number of ways. First, designers can concentrate on a smaller area and develop proportions and compositions easier than on a 360 degree surface. Second, this technique simplifies the lampmaker's work load. Once a color scheme is established, repeating pieces can all be cut at the same time. If the design repeats three times, each background piece can be cut three times.

When properly executed, a repeating design is not immediately evident. Each repeat "feeds" into the next, usually with no visible borders to designate the sectional boundaries. This creates the impression of a single, non-repeating image. A repeating design also balances the distribution of design elements on the shade. Repeats are obvious on shades whose sections are narrow and whose repeats are numerous, or where real design elements, such as vertical borders, designate and define the sections.

Weigh all these considerations when choosing a new lamp project. Make intelligent, realistic choices based on your current resources, intentions and available time. Moderation practiced in your first efforts will allow you to better absorb the many techniques that will be introduced and your new abilities will develop at a natural pace with every new lamp project.

The 18" Rose described herein was created specifically to demonstrate the design and construction techniques necessary to complete a leaded glass lamp. Dissecting (through illustration) the development of the geometric grid covering the dome section of the lamp will allow a clear and easy understanding of how the sectional aspects of lamp design are established, while the Rose design of the skirt, or lower portion, will allow the same for applying those design and construction techniques to a naturalistic rendering. It will show how these two distinct design approaches are married in a single, unifying and aesthetically pleasing theme. The distinct and easily identifiable design elements (background, foreground and borders) will facilitate a simple demonstration of glass and color selection, two very gray areas of concern for many. The shade's moderate size, 18" in diameter, conforms to what was described as a safe starting place, from which more ambitious projects can later be pursued and successfully completed.

The knowledge and understanding of these techniques will open up a world of possibilities for your stained glass work, whether you are a professional glassworker or hobbyiest. ∎

This page intentionally left blank

3

Glasses We Use

The palette of glass colors and types is rich and varied. Almost any tone, color value or textural effect can be achieved by the craftsperson who knows what's available and how best to use it.

Glass selection represents an important part of the lampmaking process. In the same way a painter prepares his palette of colors and mixes, the lamp artist must choose the correct types of colored and specialty glasses to use in the lamp's scheme. Whether the lamp is a simple geometric, a complex floral rendering, or an imaginative abstract design, skillful glass selection can make the difference between a ho-hum product and a treasure.

Translucent Vs. Opaque

It is considered undesirable to see the light source through the glass of a shade. The glare produced in glass that is too transparent to properly dissipate the light results in offensive "hot spots," distracting from the artwork on the shade. It is imperative that the natural ability of glass to transmit light is governed to allow only as much translucence as is aesthetically pleas-

ing. In most cases, it is the foreground design of the lamp that should enjoy the most attention. Background and borders should only provide backdrop and enhancement to the primary imagery. If distractions exist in either background or borders, in the form of hot spots caused by a very translucent glass, the foreground will suffer. On the other hand, if a very translucent glass is used in the primary imagery of the design, the same hot spots might distort the outline or the coloration of the image. This is also undesirable and should be remedied.

Some Tiffany lamps utilized translucent glass in background applications. Most of the time, the glass was graded from translucent to opaque, the clearest glass assembled at the top of the shade with a gradual transition to opaque toward the bottom. Even in these valuable lamps, the effect renders the shade less desirable than other Tiffany products.

The difference between translucent glass and opaque glass is very simple: If you pass your hand behind a translucent piece of glass, you will see the movement of your hand. You will not be able to see this movement through a piece of truly opaque glass.

THE LAMPMAKING HANDBOOK

Although the difference is a simple one, glasses are translucent and opaque to different degrees. One opaque glass might transmit less light than another opaque glass. Some opaque glasses transmit no light at all (such as black glass). Choosing among the different degrees of opacity is relatively simple.

Background Glass

The background areas of most lamp designs occupy the largest area of surface space. With this in mind, the difference between translucent and opaque becomes a major concern in choosing background glass. In many cases, background glass is opaque and neutral in color, allowing the greatest variety of color combinations to be employed throughout the rest of the shade. We've all seen leaded glass lamps rendered in beige, bone or almond-colored backgrounds. Besides the coloristic freedom of a neutral color, there is the clean, uniform look it provides. These colors also transmit a great amount of light, making it possible for the lamp to illuminate a large area.

Background glasses also set the tone or flavor of a shade. Obviously, a dark background will give a lamp a dramatic, heavy look, while a light background will do just the opposite. Aside from the obvious, background glasses can transmit more sophisticated and subtle effects. A spring scene, a setting sun, a brooding sky, a watery backdrop; all of these pictorial suggestions can be achieved through the intelligent selection of background glass. Introducing a fractured glass, for instance, will enhance the foreground images by suggesting activity behind. Mottled glass can suggest shadows and depth in a shade; graduated colors can simulate a changing and visually attractive sky.

Foreground Glass

Foreground is a broad term identifying the glass used for the pictorial elements of a design. Flowers, leaves, stems, tree bark, architectural images, figures, are all considered foreground elements. The selection of glasses for these differs considerably from any other part of the shade. Here, we enjoy all of the coloristic freedom our color sense allows, although choices in foreground glass may at times be governed by the background glass or the tone the background sets. For instance, a spring-like scene set by a pastel background glass will be enhanced by careful selection of contrasting, pastel foreground elements. A deep, shaded background enhances richly colored images.

Border Glass

In much the same way a picture is bordered by its frame, some lamp designs require a glass border. A border is usually comprised of uniformly sized and placed "bricks" or "blocks" of glass assembled in formation around the upper, lower and, sometimes, midsection perimeters of the lamp form. This geometric element helps unify a naturalistic design by giving the eye something structured to focus on, a rest of sorts, from the visual activity the design creates. Used most effectively on staight-bottomed lamps (as opposed to irregularly bottomed lamps), borders pictorially establish the perimeter of the lamp itself, setting the artwork off from its surrounding areas.

Border glass should relate to the main color scheme. This may mean picking up an isolated color and enhancing it or just contrasting a tone in one of the lamp's major design elements. For instance, a lamp design that incorporates light green leaves could successfully maintain borders of darker green textured glass, the texture of the glass adding interest to the borders in the same way that carving adds interest to picture frames. Thanks to an extensive selection, combinations of background, foreground and border glasses are almost limitless.

Machine-Rolled Glass

A glass made with a mechanized process instills the material with properties that can't be found in the more experimental or specialized glasses made by hand. Standardization is the greatest advantage to this kind of glass. On the technological front, standardization has helped to lower costs, speed glass production and maintain quality. Great quantities of any glass can be produced to meet demands, while consistent and reliable colors can continually be provided.

Although machine-rolled glass is not totally free of human intervention (additional colored glass may be ladled onto a base color and then mixed by experienced glass mixers to obtain multicolored effects), most of the glassmaking process for these types of glasses has been completely automated.

Almost all the processes in the creation of machine-made glasses are mechanized, including the introduction of the raw materials that are the foundation of the glass, the melting of these materials, the formation of the sheets, and the annealing (the controlled cooling) of the hot glass sheets.

Machine-rolled glass can be easily identified by the consistency of its qualities. Color, intensity, texture, thickness and mixes are consistent throughout the sheets and true to pieces made some time ago, to those available now and those that will be purchased in the future.

The availability of such a consistent product serves certain aspects of this art and craft more successfully than others. For those involved in repair and restoration, the availability of the same glasses used in the original work is a real plus. Some glasses made during the late 19th and early 20th centuries are still available through the original manufacturers, or are being reproduced by contemporary glassmakers.

On the other hand, the widespread use of these standardized colors has, to some extent, stunted the appreciation of fine colored art glass, by instilling a great deal of sameness in many of the lamps created. This is most obvious in the case of high-production lampmaking, where so many lamps, regardless of differences in design, resemble one another. These mass-produced lamps make it more difficult for the layperson to appreciate quality and excellence and to identify artistic merit and actual value where it does exist. Nonetheless, there are glassworks of merit that utilize machined glass. Through intelligent placement and knowledge of the strengths and weaknesses of the material, a craftsperson can put it to great aesthetic use.

Streakies, Wispies And Textures

Among machine-made sheet glasses, those most versatile and of greatest interest to the lampmaker are known as streakies, wispies and textures. In these three categories, the lamp artist will find color and visual effects that can add beauty and interest to any part of the art glass lamp scheme.

Streaky glass begins life as a base color, usually white, onto which streaks of a contrasting color are added. The actions of the glass mixer working with the combined glass colors, whether it be a lateral or swirling streaking, imbue the finished glass with an effect of great value to the lampmaker. Backgrounds of streaky glass can unify a color scheme if the glass incorporates colors or tones used in the other design elements of the shade. This glass can also provide a naturalistic backdrop such as sky, water, etc. Streaky glass used in the foreground can transform otherwise monochromatic images, such as flowers and leaves, into what appears to be living and breathing natural forms. Used as a border glass, streakies can highlight the surrounding areas of color with an attractive frame. Applications of this type are most popular in window schemes, and can be successfully utilized in lampmaking as long as the color choice doesn't compete with the other colors in the shade.

Wispy glass is similar to streaky glass; there

is great motion between the contrasting colors of the glass. It differs in that the base glass is usually clear, and the amount of contrasting, opaque color is reduced to allow more of the clear glass to show through. The second color, introduced by the glass mixer while the glass is still in a molten state, is governed very carefully to achieve a streakiness that is subtle yet easy to see. The wisps of color (that look very much like cloud formations when properly executed) are blended consistently throughout the entire sheet, with only occasional breaks of totally clear glass showing through.

This glass, because of its clear base, may not be as versatile to the lampmaker as streaky glass is. Yet careful placement of wispy glass can offer some pleasing effects if the clear sections are played down. A flower petal rendered in wispy glass will look more delicate than one of totally opaque glass. Since flower petals can be small in the context of an entire lampshade, a section of clear glass will not prove offensive. Where background pieces are small in comparison to the rest of the glass pieces in the design, a wispy glass might be used successfully. Here too, the small size of the glass pieces will not compromise either the overall transmission of light or the effect of the wispy glass. In border applications also, the size of the individual pieces will determine whether this type of glass is appropriate.

Textured glass has been a favorite addition to lamps since the earliest shades were built. The tactile attraction of rippling glass mounds protruding from the surrounding flat glass areas is undeniable. This high-profile glass can be one of the most pleasing in lampmaking if properly incorporated into the glass scheme.

The textures of these glasses result from glass makers manipulating the surface of molten glass with irregular motions of a roller or other texture-producing tool. The tool's surface may itself be textured or patterned in some way. The pliable, semi-hardened condition of the glass is such that the ripples and folds hold their shape through the annealing (cooling) process.

Machine-made textured glass is more uniform in profile and texture than its freely formed, hand-rolled counterpart. This is not a detraction by any means. The pattern of ripples and folds found on the machine-made product is so tightly woven into the glass surface that it is, at times, difficult to tell it from the hand-made variety. Where cost is a consideration in the planning of a particular project, the compatibility and economy of machine-made glass can prove an advantage.

Optical Qualities

Optics is the scientific study of light, its changes and the changes it produces. For our purposes, this definition can be reduced to a series of simple observations we can make by just looking at the colored glass in question.

Glass is judged and selected in one of two ways: to match a preconceived intention, such as creating a sunset or blue sky, or because of its particular beauty. In both cases, the glass' optical properties are the deciding factor in our choice. Optical quality is simply the way the glass looks with light streaming through it.

Holding a piece of machine-made glass up to a light, its greatest advantages are easily identified. The production techniques used in high-volume glassmaking deliver a consistent and reliable product.

Color value (intensity) does not vary within a single sheet, or between sheets of the same color, as much as in hand-rolled glass. This gives the glass its uniform look. Although some machine-made, three-color mixes display interesting swirls of color and movement, the overall flatness of this glass very rarely provides the depth found in its hand-rolled counterpart. This is not to say that machine-rolled glass is not beautiful and useful in itself. Quite the contrary, much of it has found its way into the most beautiful stained glass lamps. The Kokomo Opalescent Glass Company, for instance, has been making art glass since 1882, and is still making some of the same glass today. Their methods of machine-making glass have produced desirable types of glasses, including textured types that have found their way into innumerable lamps, many made by the Tiffany Studios. In fact, documentation of glass orders made by the Tiffany Studios from Kokomo have been preserved by the company.

Most non-textured, machine-made glasses transmit light very evenly. That is to say, the entire surface area of the individual glass piece is illuminated at once when lit from behind, without any variance in intensity across its surface. This property allows the maximum light to be transmitted through the individual piece of glass. Of course, darker colors allow less light to pass through. But apart from sheet-to-sheet density variations, machine-made glass should transmit light consistently throughout.

Again, this is not to say that property is totally undesirable. In cases where a lamp must provide a great deal of light to a given area, a glass with good light-transmitting ability would be most appropriate. Machine-made glass can provide that quality, often more economically and predictably than other types of glass.

Machine-made glass is physically different than more exotically produced specimens. Most obviously, it is rolled to a uniform thickness that remains true throughout the sheet and from sheet to sheet. Even the textured types of machine-made are uniform in thickness to the degree that the texture allows. One result of this property is consistent cutability of the glass. The lack of varying thickness in the material makes cutting the glass very predictable and, in most cases where the glass has been properly annealed, very easy.

Machine-made glasses are also usually available in larger sheets than the hand-rolled varieties. A hand-rolled sheet may measure 12" by 16" while a full sheet of machine-made will approach 22" by 48". These larger sheets are a result of the manufacturing process and the

continuous melting and mixing of the material along conveyor belts. The glass, after it is annealed, is cut from a long, continuous "ribbon" of glass, into the larger, narrow sheets that are made available for purchase.

There are many beautiful and interesting varieties of machine-rolled glasses that can play an important part in the scheme of a stained glass lamp. Intelligent use of these glasses broadens the palette of any lampmaker, allowing him or her to create a variety of different lamp styles.

Hand-Rolled Art Glass

In the early 1970s, a small group of glass makers began re-creating the fine art glasses of the late 19th century, including the glass made at the Tiffany Studios in New York City. This was a monumental task, because Tiffany and his glassworkers had changed the look, application and manufacturing process of sheet art glass forever. In his quest to produce a more painterly material than that available to glass artists of his time, Tiffany and his craftspeople developed new and unique ways to color and form sheet glass, all by hand. This hand rolling made the manufacture of the material an art in itself, subject to the skill and whims of the individual glassmakers. The process encouraged experimentation and individualism and resulted in a vast array of exotic glass types.

When the Tiffany Studios closed in the late 1930s, glassmaking stopped with the furnaces. The subsequent dispersal of the artisans and technicians, along with many of the formulas used in making the glass, left what had been one of the most exciting eras of American art glass without its most illustrious and seminal hosts. It would be almost 35 years before glass makers would begin to rediscover and perfect the many exotic and exciting glassmaking techniques that were practiced daily at the Tiffany Studios. Today, glass artists can enjoy a palette of glass colors and textures very much like that once available to the artists of the Tiffany Studios.

Making Hand-Rolled Glass

Where machine-made glass is a mechanized process, the making of hand-rolled glass relies heavily on individual artistry and skill. The elaborate color exchanges and surface treatments such as ripples and draperies are the result of direct manipulation of the molten glass by the glass maker. His or her abilities and experience dictate the quality, color and individuality translated into the sheet of glass. This direct and labor-intensive aspect of hand-rolled glass results in a high-quality material but also adds considerable cost to the process, which inevitably increases the price of the finished glass sheets. It is not unusual to find small sheets of hand-rolled glass that cost as much as machine-made sheets four times their size. This cost relationship may become a factor in your glass choices.

The use of machine-made versus hand-rolled has to be evaluated on a personal and aesthetic basis. You must consider the physical and artistic aspects of working these types of glass into your lamp, as well as budgetary constraints.

Computer technology has provided today's glass makers with great possibilities and advantages over early American art glass makers. Formulas, chemicals melted together to form the batch from which all types of glasses are produced, color combinations and color libraries can all be stored electronically, cataloged and cross-referenced, taking much of the hit-or-miss out of consistent quality control, as well as keeping records of those happy accidents that many times result in the most exciting glass. There's a lot to be said for this method.

The mixing of compatible and non-compatible colors into a single sheet of glass is an art in itself. This exciting type of glass provides an extensive palette of possibilities. Available from a number of glass makers, this type of glass can vary from simple, related color mixes, such as green-to-yellow streaky, to fantastic four-color mixes where one portion of the sheet is entirely different from another area.

Colors can be mixed in many ways. Some makers opt to streak and swirl the colors in specific patterns, while others prefer to freely blend and bleed color masses together, achieving the visual effect of one color gradually being transposed into another. Many manufacturers are known for their particular methods of blending colors, making their glasses highly identifiable and, in many cases, useful.

Mottled Glass

Opaque means impervious to light. Mottling varies the opacity of sheet glass on a local level, or within a very small area of the glass surface, causing blotches of dark-to-light color. Some of these blotches occupy a very small area, as in *pin-and-ring* mottling, while others carry this quality in larger *area* mottles. Mottled glass can be monochrome or multi-colored. In some cases, even textured glass has been further treated to produce mottling. This glass is the most valuable and useful when we wish to produce shadows and shading in our color scheme.

The 18" Inch Rose Border Lamp

All of the glasses chosen for the 18" Rose Border lamp are hand-rolled. The guidelines outlined here have been applied to achieve rich, yet naturalistic contrasts in all of the lamp's varied design elements.

The lamp displays the three basic elements of lamp design: foreground, background and border. The specific glass types used add interest to the relatively large areas of glass (background) and enhance the details of the smaller areas (flowers, leaves, stems and borders).

The background selection is a dense, three-color mix with scattered area mottling on a frosted base. Aqua, blue and purple contribute to the overall bluish tone of the glass, allowing the considerably large geometric area a great deal of activity even though the "grain" of the glass is linear rather than swirling in a number of directions, which would have distracted from the primary imagery of the roses. The glass is smooth on both sides.

The three geometric rows at the top, center and bottom of the lamp were cut from a low profile rippled glass that contains a similar mix of colors to the background. Its darker tone and surface texture add enough contrast to set the borders off from the background, creating a frame-like transition from the geometric grid to the naturalistic renderings of the flowers. The borders also serve to disguise the loss of the grid design behind the roses, adding much needed continuity to the design.

To achieve the layered look of the rose petals, a streaky pink-red to dark red on a frosted opaque white base was chosen. The selective mottling of the glass was used to darken the innermost areas of the petals, adding depth to the composition of the individual roses. Red contrasts very sharply with the blue of the background. When lit, there is no question where the eye should be led. The roses, being the primary image of the design, attract immediate attention. The glass is stippled.

Leaves surrounding the roses were cut from a mid-toned green-and-white glass. Mottling was used to darken those sections of the leaves closest to the roses, while the whiter areas were played down. White was used very sparingly to avoid any interference with the same color found in the rose petals. Green and red enhance each other and the greens also temper the strong contrast of flower to background glass. The glass has a stippled texture. The stems were cut from a greenish brown glass, dark enough to contrast well with the leaf glass. ∎

This page intentionally left blank

4

Tools And Equipment

The tools used in lampmaking are standard to stained glass work. Outside of the molds and template materials, no exotic machinery or implements are necessary to perform the basics involved in making a stained glass lamp. The following is a list of the basic tools needed:

- Glass cutter
- Glass breaker
- Glass grozer (optional)
- Grinder (optional but advised)
- Soldering iron (120-175 watts suggested)
- Soldering iron stand
- Wire cutters or lead snippers
- Hand-held grinding or Dremel motor tool (optional but recommended)
- Power drill with polishing pad (for finish work)

Most of the tools mentioned may be in your workshop or toolbox already. Although lampmaking does not require elaborate tools and machinery, that is not to say that none are available. The following is a list of some of the items developed to make glassworking easier and more efficient, and you might consider them as your skills improve:

- **Soldering Iron Controls (Rheostats):** Designed to better regulate the heat generated by your soldering iron. A rheostat will govern the amount of wattage available to your iron and give you critical control over the intensity of heat during soldering.

- **Alternate Grinder Bits**: Some replacement bits allow great versatility in shaping glass pieces. For example: 1/8" and 1/4" bits will reach into tighter inside curves, guaranteeing a smooth surface on all edges. Special bits for lampmaking have angled grinding surfaces to slightly bevel the glass edge, tailor the glass piece to the curved mold surface, or provide thinner spaces on inner and outer edges.

- **Eye Shield**: A simple, clear plastic attachment that mounts onto your grinder and protects your eyes and face from particles of glass that may spray from your grinding wheel. This attachment is essential.

- **Work Station Shield**: Three thin, upright plastic shields that enclose the non-working sides of your grinder, prohibiting water or glass particles from splashing around the work area.

- **Glass Grinder Foot Switch**: Frees your hands during grinding of glass pieces.

- **Glass Band Saw**: A tabletop band saw that cuts through glass easily and quickly. Good for intricate cuts through thick, textured and drapery glass. Not good for standard glass cutting as the machine's cutting speed is rather slow.

- **Lamp Holder**: A positioning tool that holds your mold or assembled lamp in any position, simplifying soldering. Though this tool can be useful, it won't work on large diameter lamps.

- **Lead-Free Solder**: 95% tin, 1% silver and 4% copper. Contains no antimony, arsenic, or cadmium. A safe solder. For those very sensitive to lead content, or concerned about exposure to lead fumes from soldering, lead-free solders offer an alternative. The added safety is reflected in the higher price.

- **Metal Bender**: A tabletop rolling machine that can form heavy brass and copper wire into large and small rings for use as reinforcement on a lampshade's aperture or straight bottom border.

- **Copper Foiling Machine**: A machine that wraps and crimps glass pieces that are hand fed into it. An excellent product that can effectively reduce foiling time, especially with a large number of geometric pieces. Not recommended for heavily textured or drapery glass.

- **Foil Dispenser**: A handy dispenser that holds a number of rolls of different sizes copper foil. Because a single lamp can incorporate glass of varying thickness, this dispenser is highly recommended. It also helps to keep foil rolls neat and stationary during foiling.

Lampmaking requires many tools and tasks with which precautions must be taken to insure health and safety. These precautions cannot be taken lightly. Some of the materials, such as solder, flux and patina can be seriously harmful if not conscientiously handled. Here is a list of some simple, yet highly recommended safety equipment for the stained glass studio:

- **Washable Work Gloves**: Keep flux from irritating skin.

- **Solvent-Resistant Gloves** (elbow length): Highly recommended when using cleaning solvents or patina solutions that contain irritants or potentially harmful chemicals.

- **Respirator With High Efficiency Cartridge**: Prevents lead fume and other metal soldering fumes from entering the respiratory system. Recommended, only if special local ventilation has not been installed for soldering operations.

- **Shop Apron**: Keeps glass fragments and staining products, such as patina solutions, off clothing. It should be washable and made of a heavy material, such as denim, that won't be damaged by heat from molten solder or a soldering iron. Special aprons of solvent resistant material should be worn when using patina solutions containing irritants or harmful chemicals.

- **Safety Goggles**: For cutting and grinding glass. Wayward glass fragments can cause eye damage. Clear plastic safety goggles are designed to protect the eyes from impact.

- **First Aid Kit and Fire Extinguisher**: For emergencies.

- **Ventilation System**: Where constant soldering is taking place. This will reduce the risk of concentrated lead and solder fumes.

For further information on safety equipment please consult Chapter 10.

Choosing A Mold

A stained glass lampshade that is spherical on any part of its surface needs to be built upon a mold, form or block (the original terminology). Its surface must be able to hold the drawn outlines of the individual pieces of glass as a permanent image. It must also provide a sturdy support for the glass during construction. It must withstand moving, storage and repeated use without falling apart or changing shape. Any material that will chip, melt, crack or become too flexible during continued studio use or storage will be inadequate for consistent professional results. The mold is the foundation upon which your artwork (lamp) is built.

Fiberglass and wood are mold materials preferable for lampmaking. Although other types of forms are available, none withstand continued use and abuse better. Full-form molds comprising 360 degrees of the form are the professional choice for lampmaking. Although sectional molds (representing only one repeat

of a given design with the design imprinted on the section's surface) are available, they cannot match the integrity of form or the ease of use of full-form molds. Sectional molds are also less accurate and, unless they are made of a superior material, less durable. Many entry level lamp forms are made of Styrofoam. Unless coated with a reinforcing material, Styrofoam bruises very easily. A simple knock will distort the form, which will distort the final result. It also reacts unfavorably to heat. The tip of hot soldering iron or a piece of molten solder will pass right through Styrofoam, leaving a gaping hole, exposing the user to toxic smoke, and compromising the mold's ability to properly support glass pieces during assembly.

Styrofoam molds are relatively inexpensive, which makes them appealing to the beginner. It has been my experience that although the cost is small in comparison to a higher quality mold, the frustrations created by the use of sectional Styrofoam molds for lampmaking are severe enough to discourage a novice. (Which makes the cost of using Styrofoam very high in terms of its value in promoting the craft.)

Plaster of Paris can be used as a mold material, although its permanence is questionable. Given plaster's tendency to chip and its overall vulnerability, it is useful only as a temporary mold material. A significant limitation of plaster is its great weight when it has and hardened into a solid mass. It can, however, be useful for creating molds of moderate size (up to 16" in diameter). Plaster is not a practical choice of mold material if a larger mold is needed; not only will the amount of plaster needed to pour a large mold be excessive, it will present serious problems when curing or hardening. Plaster is useful only when its practical limitations are understood.

Plaster can be used to make a mold from an existing work. This temporary mold is then used to obtain a contour and design outline from which a wood or fiberglass form can be created. In this case, the plaster is poured into the existing shade after its surface is treated with a release material; something that will prevent the plaster from sticking to the work and will make it easy to remove. Pouring plaster into the original accomplishes two things: First, it will accurately assume the shape of the host and, second, the lead lines on the interior of the shade will be perfectly reproduced in recess into the surface of the new mold. You can take a contour outline drawing from the new plaster, from which a wood or fiberglass mold can be fabricated. You can also trace the outline of the glass pieces, simplifying the transfer of the original design onto a new surface.

Fiberglass molds are a recent addition to the relatively short history of lampmaking; they've been available for less than 20 years. In many cases, they provide real advantages over other materials. For one, a fiberglass form is a fraction of the weight of an identical wood form, solid or hollow, making fiberglass far easier to assemble on and store.

A craftsperson will spend hours moving and positioning the lamp mold during assembly and finishing. Glass adds to the weight of the mold. Even a moderate size wooden mold of 20" can accrue a great deal of weight while in use. The weight difference between wood and fiberglass is formidable—pounds to ounces in reality. On the other hand, large molds made of fiberglass, if not properly manufactured, may be too flexible. A very large fiberglass mold will prove flimsy at its widest point and incapable of holding a true shape during use. Unless the edge of the mold is modified, fiberglass molds cannot provide a reliable working surface for extremely large diameter lamps (see Illus. 4.1).

Fiberglass does, however, clean easily, is impervious to heat and will not absorb moisture or chemicals. A simple rinsing will rid the surface of most fluxes, dirt and grease. These molds, because they are hollow, can also be stacked on top of each other, saving valuable space in the studio or workshop. They can be hung on the wall by simply drilling through the edge flange, if the mold has one, and attaching a loop or ring.

Fiberglass mold prices vary with the size, shape, makeup and treatment of the surface (carrying a pre-etched design or blank). Blank molds cast in raw fiberglass, whose surface has been polished smooth, are usually the least expensive. Next on the price scale are molds with surfaces covered in another material, usually a Gelcoat, providing a super-smooth, almost-flat, enamel-like (and preferably white) surface.

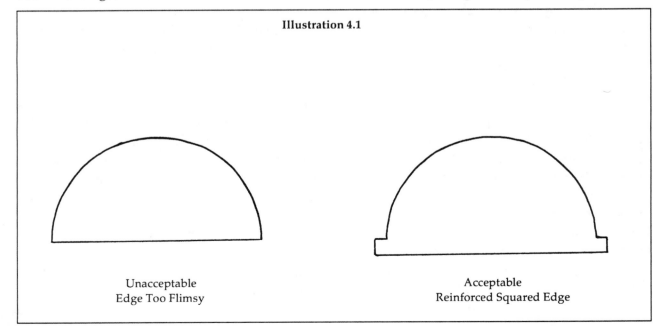

Illustration 4.1

Unacceptable
Edge Too Flimsy

Acceptable
Reinforced Squared Edge

Blank molds require the user to provide his or her own artwork.

The priciest fiberglass molds are those that have a design etched onto their surface. Although the cost of these molds may seem high, the amount of design and preparatory work they eliminate for the craftsperson justifies the expense. Molds of this type are usually packaged with a layout sheet containing the lamp's design and a copy to be cut up into templates. Designs available on prepared molds range from the simplest of geometric and Victorian styles to the most elaborate of original Tiffany lamp designs.

Wooden Molds

Wood was one of the earliest mold materials used. It provides a strong, consistent surface for lamp building. The wood form can last through many years of use. The disadvantages of wood are three: its weight, its bulk and its cost. A large mold made of solid wood can very easily weigh much more than can be comfortably manipulated in the course of lamp construction. Add to its bulk the glass and solder that become fixed to its surface in the process, and the weight can be considerable. Simply reaching around the form can sometimes be a challenge in itself, not to mention supporting it. A 28" mold has a bottom perimeter of almost 90", quite a distance around which your arms must extend. Although this must be dealt with on any large mold, regardless of material, wood's bulk and weight should be carefully considered before choosing it as a mold material. Wood molds are not available from conventional stained glass supply sources, which means that any wood mold must be first designed and then commissioned through a wood shop.

The cost of a wood mold (depending, of course, on its size, the kind of wood used and the shape of the mold) can run into hundreds of dollars. Wood turning on such a large scale is expensive and difficult and a specialized craft

in its own right. If the project at hand is a reproduction of an existing lamp, the mold used should be extremely accurate in shape and contour. Only a highly skilled woodworker or a wood shop specializing in turning large shapes will have the tools and skills to execute the form. This specialization can prove costly.

Wood molds should be turned from a wood that is accommodating to lampmaking processes. The surface must be smooth and not too porous. Even though we can seal the pores of a wood form, the less moisture the wood itself is able to absorb, the better. Moisture absorbed through the fibers of the wood will cause it to swell over time. This expansion will cause the individual lengths of laminated boards to separate at the seams. Where this occurs, moisture will continue to enter and further affect the material, compromising the accuracy of the contour and the final shape of our lamp.

Maple and poplar are two suitable woods. Both are tight-grained, delivering a smooth, hard surface that can be effectively sealed to resist moisture. Poplar, because it is an easier wood to turn on a lathe and generally less expensive than maple, is usually the better choice. In its absence, maple is preferable.

A skilled woodworker can accurately gauge the amount of wood needed based on your contour drawing (which we will discuss shortly) and be able to give you an honest estimate of the cost.

The choice of mold material should be made with all the qualities of each carefully considered. If the desired shape is commercially available in fiberglass, the choice is easy. If a particular form is not available, or an original shape is required, having it turned from wood may be the only answer.

Mold Design

A woodworker will need a contour drawing of your form to prepare the template he will use in turning the shape. A contour drawing is simply an outline of the design's edges drawn to actual size, with dimensions (height, diameter and aperture opening) displayed on the layout (see Illus. 4.2).

Along with the exterior dimensions, you must include allowances for the reinforcing hardware to be used in construction. Aperture hardware, onto which the foiled pieces of glass will be soldered and assembled, must sit in proper position at the top of the mold. The metal ring, collar, or vase cap must be positioned in the absolute center, at the top of the mold, and must be at a perfect horizontal to the overall shape. If it isn't, the finished shade will hang incorrectly or sit improperly on its base. The illustration shows how to prepare your design to meet this requirement (see Illus. 4.3):

Before drawing your contour outline, draw a straight horizontal line to represent the full diameter of the shade. For demonstration purposes, we will use a 22" length. Mark the center point (the 11" point), point A. Using a right angle, draw a straight line to represent the height of the outline (in this case 9"), perpendicular to point A, creating line B. From this perpendicular, position your right angle so that the corner meets the 9" height mark and from there draw a line parallel to the first 22" line, 2 ½" long on either side of the vertical. This represents the aperture opening (in this case, 5"), line C. You have now established perfect horizontals at the top and bottom of the outline.

Ideally, the assembled glass pieces should be seated against the aperture hardware, not above or below it. This will ensure the proper bond between glass and metal during assembly. Also, If a collar-type aperture ring is desired at the opening, a suitable recess should be designed into the mold. The collar will be seated in this recess (see Illus. 4.4).

A flexible curve is a drawing tool that allows you to create an arc or curve by bending it to the

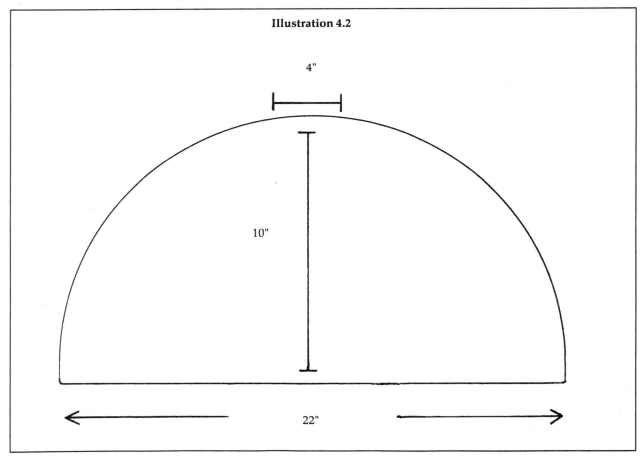

Illustration 4.2

4"

10"

22"

desired shape. It will assume the arc and remain in that position. You can then position the tool onto your drawing surface and reproduce the arc or curve by drawing against its edge. Flexible curves come in varying lengths and are available in most art supply and some office supply stores. It would be wise to purchase more than one. In the course of lamp design and layout, you will need at least two flexible curves, one 12" to 16", and one 20" to 24" long.

Using the process described above for establishing the diameter, height and aperture opening of your mold outline, you can now create any curvature you want between the edge of the aperture opening and the edge of the lower horizontal line of your drawing. Bend the flexible curve to the desired shape, place it in position on the outline and trace the curve along the edge of the tool (see Illus. 4.5).

To complete the drawing, fold it in half using the vertical line B as the central point. Fold from right to left placing the blank side of the paper over your drawing. If your paper is thin enough, you will be able to see the outline drawn earlier through the blank side. Match the horizontal lines over each other. Copy the lines onto the blank side to insure an accurate tracing (see Illus. 4.6).

Trace the outline onto the blank side, repeating the image and completing the shape. (Note that you will be tracing onto the rear of the blank side. You will need to transfer the image onto the front of the paper.) If your drawing paper is too heavy, draw and trace over a light table. This will make the lines visible through the paper and easy to reproduce.

An opaque projector is a valuable tool when re-creating an existing shape or design. This projects a full-color image of the original onto a vertical surface, such as drawing paper, from which an outline or tracing can be taken. The projected image can be scaled up or down in size, whichever suits the purpose at hand.

An opaque projector uses a beam of light to project the image onto a vertical screen, just as a slide projector does with photos. If the beam is interrupted by a solid object, such as a body, a shadow will obscure the screen. Consequently, it would be impossible to take a drawing from a projected image while standing in front of it. The drawing should be made from the rear of the projection. To do this, use a glass easel.

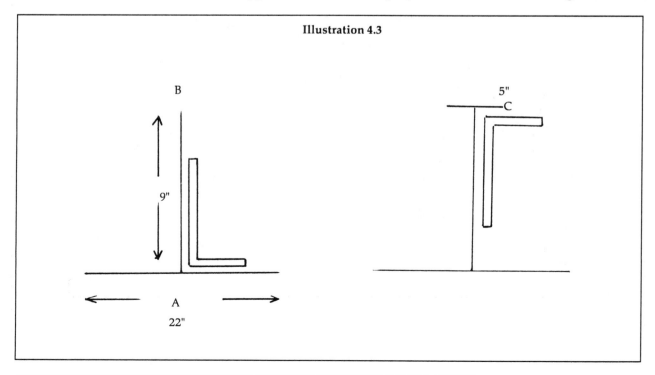

Illustration 4.3

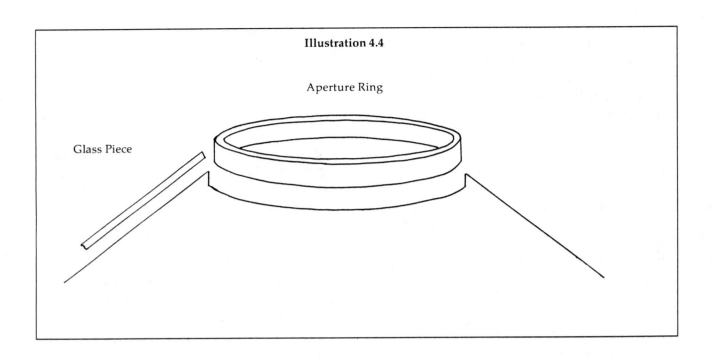

Illustration 4.4

Aperture Ring

Glass Piece

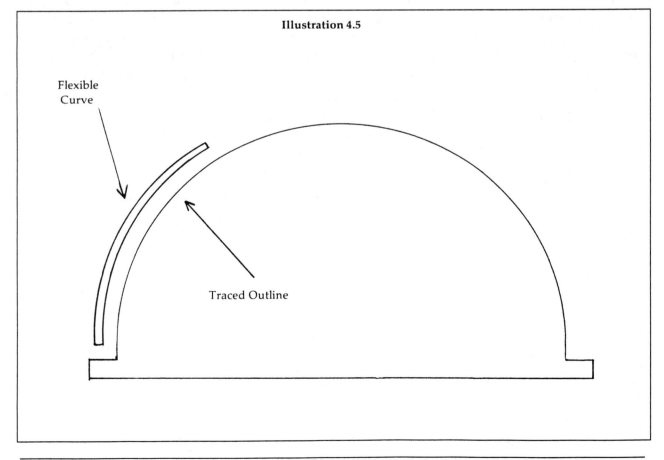

Illustration 4.5

Flexible
Curve

Traced Outline

A glass easel is simply a piece of clear glass framed and supported vertically. To make an easel suitable to our purposes, you will need a glass surface that will accommodate the largest diameter image we will be projecting (36" should suffice).

Although a standard ⅛" piece of glass would work as an easel surface, you might consider ¼" clear plate. This will provide a solid work surface upon which you can draw. You could substitute Plexiglass for the clear plate, but you might find that Plexiglass flexes or bends while you work on it; this instability may prove a distraction. Any such distraction encountered during the tracing or drawing process will compromise your ability to draw accurately.

Building a glass easel is not difficult. It is simply a piece of framed glass supported in an upright manner (see Illus. 4.7). The easel can be constructed of stock two-by-four or any size wood that will support the framed glass. The glass can be framed with channeled wood stock purchased cut to size and mitered at the corners. This framing stock is milled specifically for stained glass panels. It can also be purchased in full-length boards that you cut to size. You might want to place the easel on wheels, so that it can be moved out of the way or into a storage

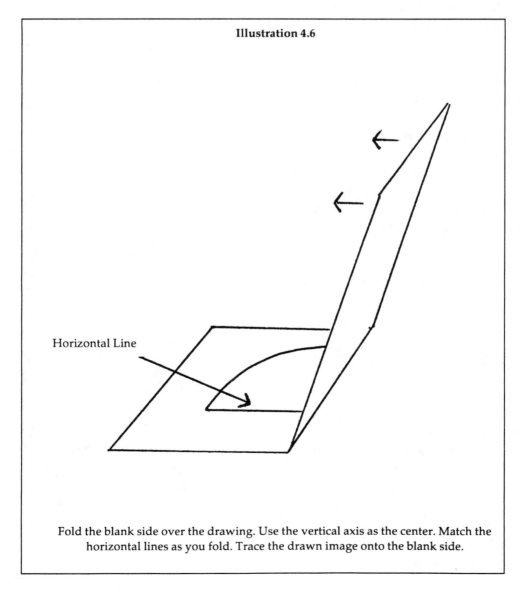

Illustration 4.6

Horizontal Line

Fold the blank side over the drawing. Use the vertical axis as the center. Match the horizontal lines as you fold. Trace the drawn image onto the blank side.

area when not in use.

Once you have chosen the image to be projected onto the glass easel and drawing surface, the transfer process is as follows:

1. Prepare your paper surface by drawing a horizontal line establishing the mold's diameter by the process described above.

2. Attach the sheet of drawing paper to the rear of the glass easel with masking tape at the corners. Make sure the horizontal guideline you've drawn is level.

3. Place the opaque projector on a flat surface, approximately as high as the lower stretcher of the glass easel.

4. Position the image to be transferred underneath the projector's lens.

5. Once you've dimmed the lights, you should be able to see the image appearing on the drawing paper. If not, move the projector until you can. The distance between projector and screen will determine the image size (see Illus. 4.8).

6. Move the projector closer or farther away from the screen until the left and right edges of the image are within the edges of your horizontal line. Once positioned, focus the image until it is sharp. You may have to alter the position of the projector again, as the image may shrink or grow as it is focused.

7. If the lamp or contour design to be recreated has a straight bottom border, match this edge with your horizontal line as carefully as possible. This will correctly position the shape. If the image has an irregular bottom border, match the left and right corner points to the left and right edges of your horizontal guideline.

8. Standing behind the screen, you should be able to transcribe the outline of the image onto your drawing paper without interfering with the projection.

Be accurate and critical when preparing your outline drawing. It is the only guide to which a moldmaker can refer. Be specific about your

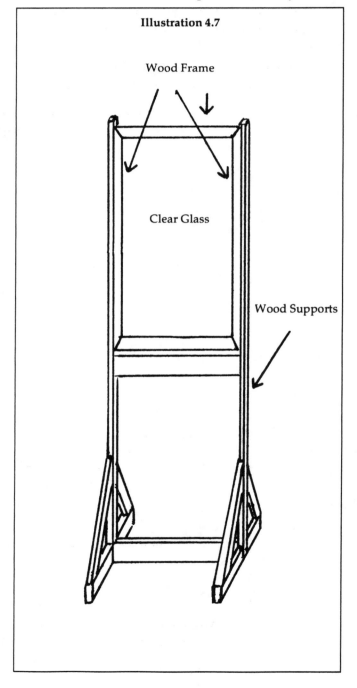

Illustration 4.7

Wood Frame

Clear Glass

Wood Supports

dimensions. He will do his best to follow your contour and design.

This projection method of design transfer is also useful when developing surface designs.

Templates

A template is an accurate, physical replica of an outlined space on the surface of the lamp mold. It will facilitate cutting of the shape in glass, and fitting the resulting piece into place. Templates should be perfectly flat, made of a relatively durable material (one that will allow a glass cutter to rest against it during a score) and be a true representation of its corresponding glass space on the mold in size, shape and detail. Anything less will lead to inexact results.

The material used for templates varies with the purpose at hand. If you plan to make only one lamp from the templates you will be preparing, it is not necessary to cut and hone them from sheet metal, for instance. You can prepare suitable templates from a variety of materials, including paper, plastic acetate or mylar.

Preparing patterns for a complex lamp with many pieces can be a time-consuming affair. The result should justify the expense of time. Metal templates are the most durable and will withstand constant handling over a long period, without showing any signs of deteriora-

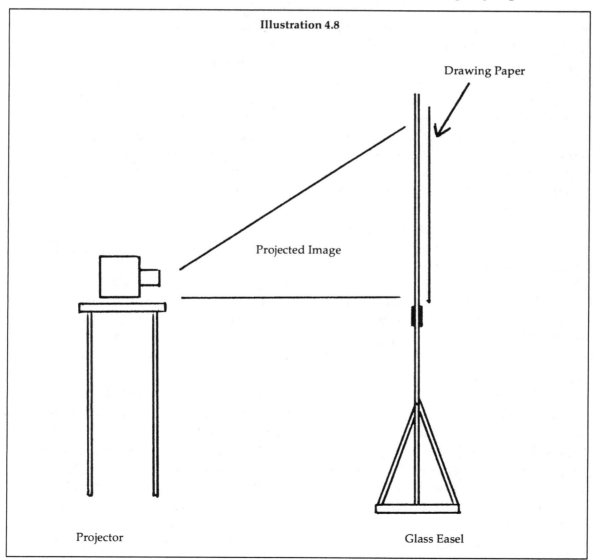

Illustration 4.8

Drawing Paper

Projected Image

Projector

Glass Easel

tion. They provide a solid and dependable edge against which the glass cutter can travel. In studio situations, where glass cutting is delegated to craftspeople of varying abilities, metal pattern shapes insure greater accuracy. Metal templates can also be taken to the glass grinder and used over and over to ensure accuracy when shaping pieces of glass and honing them to perfection. Unlike paper patterns, the integrity of the metal shape will not be compromised by its contact with water.

Paper and plastic (mylar) templates are by far the easiest to prepare. The material can be cut and shaped simply with a pair of scissors. If a pattern is lost or damaged, it can be replaced in a matter of minutes, in contrast to the time it would take to duplicate the same piece in metal. Preparing paper templates for an entire lamp is also far less time consuming.

While easier to create, paper or mylar templates must be handled carefully. Paper damages easily, especially when scoring against it with a glass cutter. The wheel of the cutter can cut right into the shape and shear off the edge of the paper with less pressure than is needed to score the glass. Once damaged, the template must be replaced.

Paper folds easily. A creased pattern piece is very difficult to flatten against the glass, and troublesome to work with. Such pattern pieces need be replaced.

In chapter seven, transferring the lamp design onto templates drawn on masking tape is discussed. The masking tape is pressed onto paper or mylar, augmenting the material and increasing its durability. With the proper care, pattern pieces prepared in this way can last almost indefinitely.

Whatever template material you choose, it must allow the glass cutter's wheel to spin freely against the glass. Glass cutters have less than the full radius of the cutting wheel exposed at the end of the tool. The distance between the edge of the wheel and the housing securing the wheel is where the template butts against the wheel during a score. If the template is too thick, the scoring edge of the wheel will not reach the glass (see Illus. 4.9). Check your template material first to ensure that this isn't the case.

Other practical considerations will influence your choice of template materials. Obviously, a softer material, such as a plastic acetate, will be easier to shape than a harder one, such as sheet metal. An easier material will also take less time to prepare. (One suggestion if you choose mylar for templates: Use frosted white or opaque. The templates and their outlines will be easier to see. Clear templates are easy to lose.)

In some elaborate lamps, template making can seem an endless drudgery. On the other hand, given the reliability and accuracy of more durable patterns of a harder material, you will be better prepared to achieve consistent, professional results every time.

In the course of this book, you will be following the 18" Rose Border lamp through its design, the preparation of its templates and its fabrication. For our demonstration, we will be using templates made from masking tape backed with mylar. More than likely, you will encounter such templates whether you build from a kit or choose to design your own.

Staples: Copper Foil, Solder, Flux

Every project in stained glass requires the use of certain studio staples. Solder and flux are necessary to join glass pieces whether they are framed in copper foil or lead, and whether the work is a flat panel or a curvilinear lamp.

Copper Foil

Copper foil is the edging material of choice for most lamps. Traditionally, copper foil allows greater depiction of detail in design and glass selection, due to its flexibility. Copper foil can easily be wrapped around the smallest pieces of glass. Although lead came can be used in lampmaking, its bulk and inflexibility limit its practical applications. For the purposes of this book, all glass pieces were wrapped in copper foil.

Copper foil with a prepared adhesive backing is a relatively new addition to the battery of stained glass tools. As recently as 20 years ago, stained glass craftsmen were making their own by slicing sheet foil to size and applying a spray adhesive to the rear. Earlier lampmakers prepared their sheet foil with a backing of beeswax. The convenience of having foil pre-cut to various widths and prepared with an adhesive backing was a boon to the craft.

The introduction of prepared copper foil also provided glassworkers with convenient rolls cut to standard widths. The most popular diameters from thinnest to widest are: 5/32", 3/16",

7/32" and 1/4". The diameter should correspond to the thickness of the glass to be wrapped (thin foil for thinner glass, and thicker foils on thicker and textured glassses.)

Certain pieces of very thin or very wide glass will require odd sizes of copper foil, available by special request (1/8" and 1/2" foil, for instance). For very thick glass, it is possible and quite practical to double foil with a standard width to achieve a wider foil face (see Illus. 4.10). Most foil is packaged in 36-yard rolls.

The actual thickness of the copper foil is measured in millimeters, and is sold according to this specification. Some foils can be purchased in a thickness as fractional as .001 millimeters.

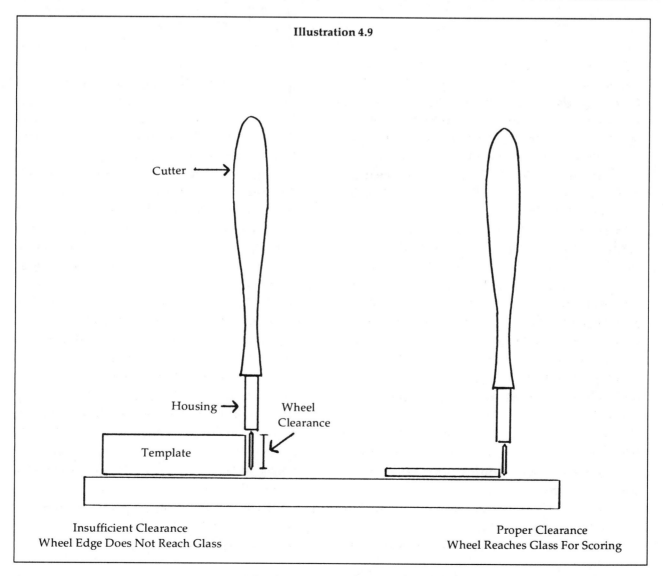

Illustration 4.9

Cutter

Housing →

Wheel Clearance

Template

Insufficient Clearance
Wheel Edge Does Not Reach Glass

Proper Clearance
Wheel Reaches Glass For Scoring

It is best to check with your supplier and try each thickness for yourself, choosing the one most comfortable to work with (see Illus. 4.11).

Solder

Solder bonds our foiled glass pieces to each other and to whatever metal reinforcing materials we choose to add to the work. The most common configurations of lead/tin solders available to the stained glass craftsman are 50/50 and 60/40. These numbers represent the ratio of tin to lead in the individual rolls (the first number represents the percentage of tin).

Lead content retards the melting of the solder, making a 50/50 solder a bit slower in reacting to heat from a soldering iron than 60/40. It will prove *gummier* than a solder containing more tin. More heat from the soldering iron will speed up the melting of a lead-heavy solder, but will never increase its efficiency over a 60/40 solder used under the same circumstances. Less tin also hinders the solder's ability to accept metal coloring agents, or patina. This can be a serious problem in certain cases.

On the plus side, 50/50 solder is less expensive than 60/40. Raw tin is prone to wide price swings in the industrial metals market. These vagaries are reflected in the price of all lead/tin solders and are all too common to those who purchase them regularly. Stained glass artists, craftspeople and shop owners know only too well how the price of solders can fluctuate on an almost daily basis. Smart buyers purchase in bulk when price levels are favorable.

A 60/40 solder is preferable for fine lamp-making. Its low melting point, relative purity and ability to accept patina (given the higher integrity of its tin content), make it conducive to better results. The 50/50 solders are not impossible to work with. Good results can be had with them, but they require more work and, in some cases, more time.

Lead-free solder has recently become widely available to the stained glass industry. Lead is a toxic material; its presence in the workplace warrants special safety precautions whenever it is used. Lead is a cumulative toxin. Repeated use of lead materials without taking proper precautions can result in a buildup of lead in the body. This absorbed lead can cause kidney and nervous system problems ranging from psychological disturbances to dimensia and paralysis. Some symptoms may develop only after years of exposure. It is also a potent reproductive hazard. Lead-free solders are just what they propose to be...lead free. Lead-free solders are much safe provided they do not contain arsenic, antimony or cadmium. Those made from tin, zinc, silver bismuth and copper are among the safest. Although it doesn't flow as smoothly as 60/40 solder, the increased safety is well worth the trade off. Be ready to spend more for lead-free solder on a per roll basis: safety has its price.

It is a good practice to shop around, as the price of solder can fluctuate in a roller-coaster fashion. If your budget allows, do not hesitate to take advantage of attractive solder prices sometimes offered for bulk purchases. These sales are often short-lived and represent a special arrangement made possible by your supplier and the solder manufacturer, or distributor. Savings of even a few pennies per pound can multiply into a sizable amount when solder is purchased in quantity. A large lamp can easily require eight to ten pounds of solder and maybe more, if the fit of the glass pieces is loose. Solder, in these cases, becomes a serious expense and should be considered carefully.

Capping bars are solid sticks of solder that, in some cases, may prove more economical than roll solder. Capping Bars are usually 3/16" to 1/2" square rods approximately one foot long. They are available only through solder-producing metals manufacturers, not from stained glass suppliers. When pricing solder for quantity purchase, it is wise to look into these bars; you may find the costs to be competitive. For the names of suppliers of capping bars, look in the Yellow Pages under "Metals."

Because capping bars do not have to be

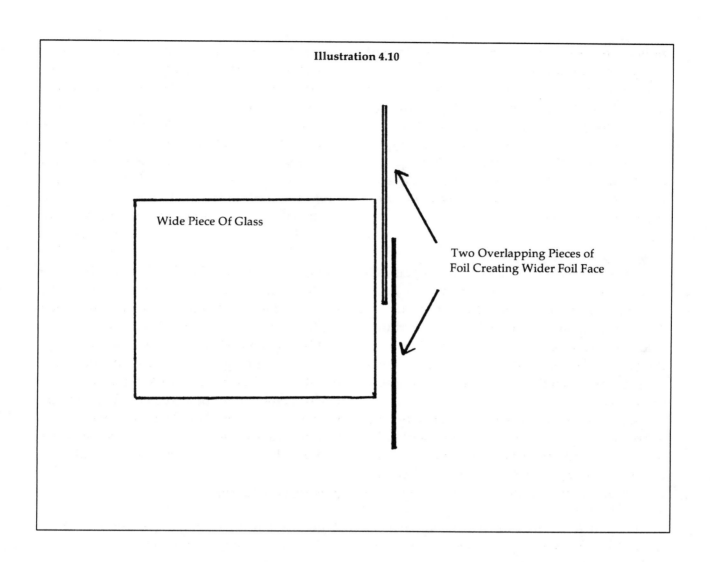

Illustration 4.10

Wide Piece Of Glass

Two Overlapping Pieces of
Foil Creating Wider Foil Face

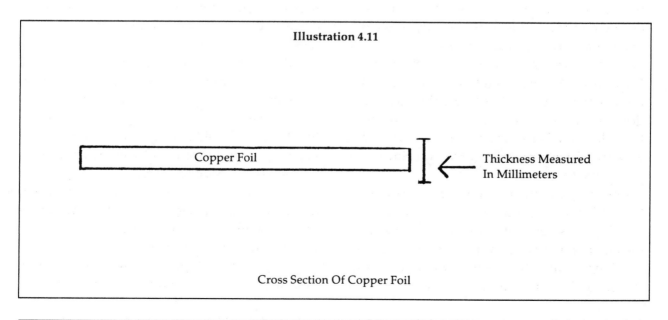

Illustration 4.11

Copper Foil

Thickness Measured
In Millimeters

Cross Section Of Copper Foil

pulled from a spool, they can be very efficient for lampmaking. During soldering, spool solders need to be constantly unwound to extend the wire of solder. One must stop soldering, unwind the solder using both hands and continue. Although this movement is second nature to most craftspeople, it does eat up quite a bit of time during the finish soldering of a large work. When a capping bar is used up, you simply pick up another.

Flux

Flux acts as a catalyst between the metal materials to be joined and the substance used to join them. The application of flux to a surface performs a double function. First, being mildly acidic, it cleanses the surface, preparing it for the solder. Second, it slightly lowers the temperature at which the metal will readily accept the solder.

Flux is applied to the surface sparingly with a short-bristled brush. Since flux is subject to the heat of the soldering iron, it evaporates rather quickly during construction, making the wholesale fluxing of an entire piece unnecessary and wasteful.

Paste and liquid fluxes are the most commonly used in lampmaking. There are advantages and disadvantages to both. Paste flux, because of its jelly-like consistency, is highly stable and can be more carefully and critically applied to the work surface. Because of its consistency, paste flux will not "pop" or "spit" as liquid fluxes do, when exposed to the intense heat of the soldering iron. Unlike liquid flux, paste flux does not cause as many *fisheyes* or pinholes on the solder line's surface during soldering. The absence of these imperfections saves time spent correcting them.

Certain paste fluxes, however, have a nasty habit of leaving a film on the metal and glass, one that does not easily rinse off. In some cases, the residue will not be apparent until the lamp is being prepared for patina. Any residual substance will compromise the effectiveness of metal coloring agents. It then becomes necessary to re-clean the lamp and possibly requires the use of an abrasive (steel wool) to remove the remaining paste flux.

Liquid fluxes are clear and watery in consistency. They are applied in the same way as paste fluxes but, because of their consistency, have a tendency to be messy. Liquid fluxes can find their way onto and into anything in the studio. Because a mildly acidic solution, flux has oxidizing properties. This means that any metal objects, such as tools and supplies, that come into contact with the flux will begin to oxidize (rust). If they are not rescued from the reaction, they will continue to oxidize until they are totally rusted and completely useless.

It is best to purchase fluxes prepared specifically for stained glass work. Stained glass distributors and suppliers stock these products. Good fluxes should be easy and relatively safe to work with. They should be completely water soluble to allow total removal from all the glass and metal once soldering has been completed.

Soldering Irons

A good soldering iron delivers consistent heat and, given proper care, should provide long service. The successful construction of a lamp depends upon reliable performance from a soldering iron. One of high quality, in a size (wattage) that matches the craftsperson's abilities and the requirements of the job, will greatly aid assembly and finishing. The speed and consistency of heat from your soldering iron governs the efficient and speedy completion of a lamp. Ideally, you should solder with the hottest iron you can comfortably and efficiently control.

Choose a soldering iron carefully. Price should not be the determining factor, when deciding on a wattage or quality. The choice should be made based upon the purposes for which you will use the iron.

With the many types of irons available, it is essential to distinguish the good from the bad.

For instance, a soldering iron of modular design, one whose parts (element, handle, casing, wire and tip) can easily be replaced if damaged or worn, may initially be more expensive. In the long run, however, this iron will prove more cost efficient than a lower priced one that can only be discarded when it has run its useful course or trouble develops.

Some irons are shipped with tips (usually copper) that are not plated. Plating prevents the surface from deteriorating and breaking down in reaction to the consistently high heat generated by the element during extended work sessions. Non-plated tips must be replaced. Plated tips are available in a number of different shank sizes and shapes. Better irons are shipped with plated tips already installed.

Inexpensive irons of suspiciously high wattage may deliver impressive amounts of heat initially, only to simmer down after a short time. Such cooling will slow a craftsperson's work considerably and, of course, add time to the project. Consequently, these "bargain" irons should be avoided.

Most irons cannot deliver eight hours of constant heat on a daily basis for very long without showing some wear and tear. Proper care and maintenance of the tool is required to ensure dependable use. Studios, especially those with soldering departments or craftspeople who function specifically as solderers, need tools that can perform reliably day after day. Here, the soldering equipment must produce even and consistent heat to facilitate quick, efficient assembly and finishing. A reliable, properly maintained soldering iron is a necessity in such an environment. Wise craftspeople weigh the value of an iron based on its performance as a production tool and not its cost in dollars.

The choice of a soldering iron should be an intelligent one. A craftsperson should not use an iron that exceeds or limits his or her ability to control its heat. A hot iron requires quick responses and good working speed from its operator. On the other hand, a cool iron in the hands of an experienced solderer will frustrate him or her by not delivering sufficient heat when it is needed.

If you are new to the craft or are training a beginner, a moderate size iron of 100 to 120 watts will provide adequate heat for lampmaking without overwhelming your skill. Larger or hotter irons melt solder very quickly, making it thinner and harder to control as the applied heat increases. This is true whether joining metals or leading a network of copper foiled glass. If the solder is melting faster than it can be controlled, an even bead (lead line) cannot be created. Repeated attempts to re-work an area that is proving troublesome because of this, may cause too much heat to build up in one spot. As it becomes thinner, the solder runs through the lead line onto the rear of the work. The increased heat can also create cracks in the glass called heat cracks.

You should not use a high-wattage soldering iron until you are proficient in controlling moderate amounts of heat. Any upgrade will then be comfortable, manageable and safe for your glassworking projects.

Irons of 175 to 200 watts are the professional's choice for lampmaking. The intense heat generated by these irons will help a skilled craftsperson speed through assembly, reinforcing and finishing. Some craftspeople use two irons to finish larger shades. While one is dispensing heat during soldering, the other is building up heat to replace the first when it begins to cool and slow down.

You should not attempt to use either a very hot iron or two irons at once until your skills warrant it. If you feel your soldering iron is holding you back, it may be that your skill has outgrown your small iron and it is time to move up. An iron of 100 to 120 watts is best for beginning lampmakers. These irons will deliver sufficient amounts of consistent heat for all lampmaking needs, and can be easily controlled. If you find either of these to be more than you can comfortably use, consider a rheostat, or temperature control to govern the generated heat. Gradually increase the wattage as your skills improve.

Having made your choice of soldering iron, it is important to know how to care for it. Proper cleaning and maintenance of the iron will prolong its life, returning many times its initial cost in actual service.

Soldering Iron Maintenance

The most vulnerable part of the soldering iron is the tip. Heat is concentrated at its point. Solder is applied at its edge. The tip encounters any dirt or residue on the lead lines or in the solder itself. It also attracts dirt from the surrounding atmosphere and oxidizes. The resulting residue builds up on its surface. Any time you leave your soldering iron unattended and plugged in, it will sit and "cook." When you return, a crust of dirt will have accumulated on the tip. A quick pass with a wire brush will remove most of the dirt from the tip, unless the iron is left to cool without cleaning. The accumulated crust will then solidify on the tip. If this is allowed to happen regularly, the dirt will build up around the surface of the tip enclosed by the iron's sleeve, causing it to freeze or fuse to the sleeve. This will make it very difficult or even impossible to remove. If a soldering tip cannot be removed for cleaning, it will continue to accumulate this crust on its surface, most notably at the joint of tip and sleeve. Although the iron will still heat up and function, its life has been limited to that of the tip which will eventually split, at which point the entire unit will be rendered useless. This is a major cause of many soldering irons' demise.

Care of your iron is a relatively simple matter. If practiced from the start and on a regular basis, this maintenance will become routine. Here are a few suggestions that will aid in prolonging the studio life of your soldering irons:

1. Never leave your iron on and unattended for long periods of time. Besides the obvious excess wear and tear, this is a safety hazard.

2. Keep the tip as clean as possible when in use; frequently wipe the tip with a cleaning agent, such as a soldering sponge. When cleaning the tip with flux, never dip it further than ½" into the liquid. Flux should not be allowed to seep into the sleeve holding the tip. Flux is an acid and can prove harmful if not handled carefully.

3. Hold and move your iron in a "tip down" position, to prevent any flux or liquid residue from traveling down the tip into the sleeve where it can cool, solidify and cause the tip to freeze up. Special soldering iron caddies are available to hold the iron in this position when it is not being used (see Illus. 4.12).

4. Where less than the iron's full heat is needed, use a rheostat or external control to govern the temperature. There's no need to waste energy.

5. Remove accumulated grime from the tip of the iron. Brush the tip quickly and briskly with a wire brush. Brushing should be done away from the body to avoid being burned by the falling bits of dirt.

6. At the end of the day, remove the soldering tip from the iron and brush it clean with a wire brush. Hold the tip with a pair of pliers and brush it clean. Pay special attention to the iron's set screw. Keep it lubricated and free of corrosion, and working smoothly at all times..

7. Keep spare irons and tips on hand.

8. Always unplug your iron at the end of your work session.

Reinforcing Materials

A lamp's network of solder lines forms a metal framework, or skeleton, holding the foiled glass pieces together. Some large lamps, due to their increased diameters, must have this metal network supplemented or reinforced. As the expanse of glass increases, so does its vulnerability, especially at the expanding outer edges. Special hardware and materials are used to strengthen the glass shape at various locations in the structure.

Lamps of any size must be constructed with proper reinforcement; good craftsmanship demands it. At the very least, a collar or ring of substantial size in relation to the diameter and depth of the shade should be installed at the aperture, and a finished border of brass or copper wire must be installed along the bottom edge. Reinforcement at these locations

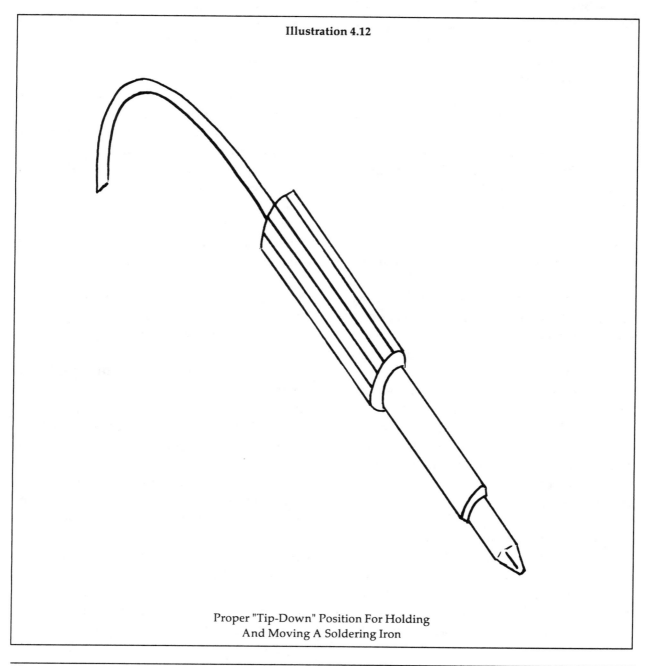

Illustration 4.12

Proper "Tip-Down" Position For Holding
And Moving A Soldering Iron

THE LAMPMAKING HANDBOOK

strengthens the shape significantly. This is a necessity for the shade's longevity and endurance to being moved.

The popular practice of finishing the edge of a stained glass lamp with a bead of solder melted onto the edge of the exposed copper foil does nothing for the strength of a shade. It reinforces the foil, not the shade. As the expanse of a shade increases, so does the vulnerability of the shade's edge. Without reinforcement, even a gentle bump from any direction can result in damage to the border glass or the integrity of the form. Similarly, soldering a brass vase cap directly to an aperture opening that has not been previously reinforced, leaves the brass cap and the underlying thin copper foil bearing the downward gravitational weight of the entire shade. This practice often leads to a separation of the cap from the aperture opening. Accumulated heat rising from the light bulbs is captured in the upper section of the shade, causing a gradual softening of the solder and subsequent loosening of the thin brass cap from the aperture opening. Heat cannot disrupt a ring or collar of appropriate thickness that has been securely fixed to the aperture opening. If properly applied, the mass of metal requires more heat than the bulbs can generate to soften the solder joints. Only in very rare cases, where the wattage of the light bulbs is unusually high, will there be any risk of damage.

It is interesting to note that even the earliest lamps of the Tiffany Studios (pre-1900) were properly reinforced. A cast 1/8" by 1/2" solid brass ring or collar was soldered to the aperture, while a brass wire ring of similar thickness was soldered to the bottom edge. In the case of irregular bottom borders, a thinner, more flexible wire was attached to the glass, following its every curve. Interiors of larger lamps were further reinforced with wires soldered onto existing lead lines. They were installed vertically (four to six equally spaced wires extended from the aperture to the bottom border) and sometimes horizontally (a single wire installed approximately two inches above the bottom border, following the lead lines around the inside perimeter of the shade).

Tiffany's reinforcement techniques were standard practice for the many years the studio produced lamps. Lamp hardware, developed in concert with their bronze bases to insure a solid support system, consisted of collars ranging in size from 2" to 6" in diameter. The smallest were simple rings of metal, the largest, more elaborate castings. The intact survival of so many of Tiffany's leaded glass shades bears testimony to the effectiveness of the studio's construction methods and reinforcement techniques. We can use and adopt similar materials and techniques today, confident in their reliability and appropriateness.

Stained glass shades 20" in diameter and less were fit with aperture rings and edge reinforcement only. No wires were attached to the interior of these shades. The close and relatively small network of glass pieces and solder lines provided enough strength to forego any additional reinforcment. This is evident when handling any of these shades; they feel very sturdy and solid. Those without a bottom border, on the other hand, feel flimsy in comparison, their edges will respond to the slightest exterior pressure by bowing and flexing. Lamps larger than 20" were reinforced on the interior with wire, in addition to the standard aperture and border treatments. The most elaborate and complex designs, such as the Wisteria and Laburnum, were substantially reinforced from within. These complex designs include long, narrow clusters of small copper foiled glass pieces extending up to 2" below the greater massing of glass. Such sections were very vulnerable and susceptible to damage. The reinforcement wires installed in these shades formed a structural network in themselves, providing the extra support the shades needed.

When planning any lamp project, proper reinforcement and structural considerations must be included in the preliminary stages. If you intend to reproduce an existing design using an available kit, suitable hardware is more than likely available from the same source. Certain manufacturers of lamp-building systems provide the appropriate hardware along with their design and lamp-building aids.

Aperture rings can be adapted to situations where their easy installation has not been provided. Because an aperture ring has no ⅜" center opening by which it can be secured to a threaded nipple at the top of a lamp form, it cannot be secured, or anchored to the top of a mold in the same way as a brass cap can. In such cases, a brass vase cape the same size as the ring is used during assembly. The ring is installed later, replacing the cap once the cap has been removed, or melted out, from the opening. In some cases, if the aperture opening has first been strengthened with a brass channel or wire, the vase cap can remain, provided it is properly fused to the channel or wire by solder.

Reinforcement wires are used to strengthen the inner structure of larger lamps and as an edging material for irregularly shaped bottom borders. The interior wires, installed after final leading, are soldered to existing lead lines, effectively increasing the shade's strength.

The wires generally used for this purpose are 14- and 16-gauge reinforcement wires. Brass, because of its higher tensile strength, is favored over copper wire. Copper, on the other hand, is softer and more accommodating to the intricate bends reinforcement wire must assume when being soldered to existing lead lines. Copper conducts heat faster and holds it longer than brass, making handling it, at times, tricky.

The size difference between 14- and 16-gauge wire is minimal and a matter of choice. Both are suitable. It is important to note that the gauge number decreases as the diameter of the wire increases. Thus, 14 gauge is thicker and less flexible than 16 gauge. To ensure the highest degree of reinforcement, the strongest wire should be used: 14-gauge. Where this gauge proves too difficult to work with, as in a highly

irregular bottom border, 16-gauge will suffice. Much thinner gauges offer little value as reinforcement, and much thicker gauges will prove too difficult to bend.

Reinforcement brass and copper wire is packaged in rolls. The most common rolls contain approximately 15' of wire. Although most brass and copper wire can be found at hardware stores and home centers, the heavier gauges cannot. Stained glass suppliers and hobby and craft centers are a better source for these materials. They can be special ordered if necessary.

Patina Solutions And Finishing Waxes

All lampmakers are fond of a specific type of patina and finish for their works. It might be the popular greenish-bronze of original Tiffany lamps, a reddish copper brown, a brownish-black or even a highly polished golden-copper. Whatever the preference, a well-stocked studio should have a selection of patina solutions ready to accommodate any need.

These solutions need not be stored in great quantities unless, of course, they are used in great quantities. Individual lampmakers who do not apply patina on a daily basis should keep a small but practical amount of these solutions on hand. Suppliers generally carry these in pints, quarts and gallons. Local stained glass suppliers and hobby stores will stock only those that are most popular in the craft. More specialized solutions will have to be ordered or obtained from larger supply houses or specialty firms. The following is a list of the solutions lampmakers should be familiar with:

Copper Sulfate
Available in liquid or crystal form (crystals dissolved in water allow the craftsperson to mix his or her own solution to any strength as the need arises). Copper sulfate is a very popular coloring agent. It imparts a copper-gold finish onto the lead lines. The metal needs only to be cleaned to react properly with the solution.

Copper Plating Solution

Available in pre-mixed liquid form. This solution effectively plates the base metal with a copper-orange color very close to that achieved by the more elaborate and specialized process of electroplating. The presence of sulfuric acid in the solution demands special safety precautions be taken when using this liquid.

Brown Darkener

Available in liquid form, this is a clear solution that will gradually darken the base metal to a brown tint. It is most effective on brass, copper, bronze and copper-plated lead/tin solder.

Brown Black Darkener

Also available in liquid form, this clear solution produces a darker brown color, approaching black. It is most effective on brass, copper, bronze and copper plated lead/tin solders.

Pewter Finish

A clear, liquid solution that produces a charcoal grey color on brass, copper, bronze and lead/tin solders. Solder need not be plated to accept this color.

Black Patina

This clear liquid effectively blackens the base metal. It works on copper, brass, bronze, copper plated and non-plated lead/tin solders. It also blackens zinc.

Green Patina

This blue-green liquid, when properly applied, simulates the effects of oxidation on the base metal. It is effective on brass, copper and bronze. It will react to lead/tin solders only if they have been chemically or electrically copper plated. A fine green patina has always been the most elusive of metal finishes. Proper cleaning and preparation of the base metal is of paramount importance when using solutions of this type. Because the greening of the metal is a cumulative process, it is the most time-consuming step and the one most susceptible to environmental conditions and variable results.

Blue-Green Patina

This liquid patina is very similar to green, producing an interesting turquoise rather than a yellow-green finish.

Finishing Waxes

A fine patina profits from waxing. It highlights the treated metal and prevents further oxidation where no lacquer sealant has been applied. Most brands of paste wax for furniture applications work well when polishing both glass and metal. No abrasive waxes should ever be used on works which have been treated with patina solutions. The abrasive will damage the patina. Applying these metal coloring agents will be discussed in chapter Seven. ■

5

Preparation

Practicality and convenience should govern the arrangement of your workspace. Tools, equipment and supplies must be located where you want them when you want them. Parts that have limited use during your lampmaking, such as lamp molds, need to be stored when not in use. Items such as the glass grinder and light table, which you will turn to and away from many times in the course of your lamp building, need to be positioned close by. If they are not, effort and time will be wasted in traveling from point to point.

An effective "work triangle" should be established in the workspace. All of the activities associated with the assembly and finishing of a lamp can be done within this area. Ideally, each station should be no further than three comfortable steps away from any other working area within the triangle (see Illus. 5.1).

The three components of our work triangle are a worktable, a light table and a grinder station. These are all simple structures that can be easily built with a minimum of tools and woodworking abilities, or they can be purchased fairly inexpensively. Whichever you choose, you will need these three elements.

Worktable

The most common size for worktables is 4' by 8'. This measurement coincides with the size of most plywood sheets as they are stocked at the lumber yard. No further cutting or sizing of these large and clumsy sheets is needed. If you already have a functional work table or just want to buy one of the many available from home building centers, skip this section. For the true do-it-yourselfer, though, I include here instructions on making your own worktable and light table.

Light Table

A light table or light box of some sort is necessary for fine lampmaking. In choosing glass and laying out the cut and ground pieces of the design, it is imperative that you see what the final effect of your choices will be. You must determine how effective color combinations and painterly effects such as shading and color transitions will be. You can purchase a small light table at an art supply store, which may be the best alternative for the beginner. Instruc-

Illustration 5.1

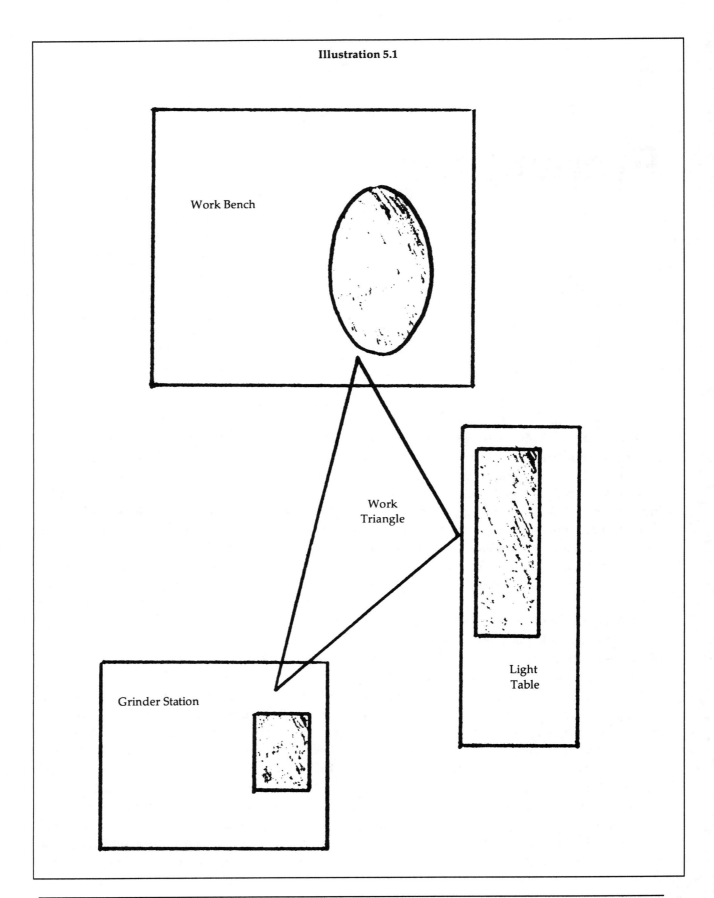

tions for building a light table are included here for the do-it-yourselfer or motivated craftsperson.

Grinder Station

Your glass grinder needs to be near your light table. When cutting glass, it is a good idea to grind and place the glass pieces onto the lamp layout as soon as possible. Patterns and glass pieces have a peculiar habit of disappearing when left loose or stacked up. If the work triangle is set up similar to the diagram, moving to and from these positions should never take more than three natural steps.

A grinder should sit on a surface as high as your worktable; no special structure is necessary. Whatever is chosen to support a grinder station should have a large enough work area for the grinder and some open surface area on both sides to accommodate glass pieces and any other items you might use while grinding, such as a basin of clear water for rinsing glass, or paper towels for drying the pieces.

Storage

Space is truly a luxury. Few artists and craftspeople enjoy an abundance of it, and most have to make do with limited amounts. Clever use of studio space maximizes the ease and comfort of how we conduct our workday rituals of preparation and creation. Studios and individual lampmakers share their work areas with two space-hungry tenants: glass and lamp molds.

Glass

Glass storage is a complex consideration because of the delicate nature of the material and the odd-sized sheets and pieces craftspeople tend to keep on hand. It is not uncommon to find a lampmaker's studio littered with crates containing small pieces of glass that other studios (not involved with lampmaking) would

dispose of. Given the small size of some lamp pieces and the great value of some of the more exotic and unique types of handmade glasses, this hoarding is justified. On the practical side, however, it calls for a storage solution. Cubic airspace is probably the most overlooked of all storage areas in the studio. Anything that can be stacked, should be.

Glass sheets should be stored vertically, not in cardboard boxes or laying flat in piles. Large sheets should be stored in racks or bins resembling the crates in which they were shipped. Smaller sheets and fragments should be kept in crates that can be stacked with their open end facing out for easy access. You may be able to obtain empty glass crates from your local supplier. If they store their glass in prepared racks, they may have shipping crates available. If so, the crates can be useful as vertical storage bins lined up side by side in the studio. Ask about costs. (These crates should never be stacked on top of one another.)

As the pieces of glass get smaller, the storage problem becomes more complex. Where and how do you store the smallest pieces and what size piece should ultimately be disposed of? To the first half of the question, practical and general solutions can be found. The answer to the second is more subjective.

If space, time and money allow, storage compartments can be built to accommodate graduated sizes of glass. Each section will house a certain size sheet and each compartment a certain color (see Illus. 5.2). They should not be too deep. The deeper the compartment, the greater the probability of scrap glass getting lost in the rear (having to reach too far into a rack can also be dangerous). All storage compartments should have smooth bottoms and sides. Small glass fragments will find their way into any crevices, creating a potential hazard. Many glass related accidents occur while searching for and moving glass around the studio. If you limit the opportunities for fragmented glass to accumulate in out-of-the-way areas, you also cut down the potential for those accidents.

Consider the great weight these racks will support. A small piece of glass does not weigh much in itself, but put hundreds of them together and the weight becomes formidable. Professional help should be sought if building glass racks is out of your sphere of experience or ability. The money spent on an experienced carpenter represents an investment in adequate and efficient storage. Visit other glass studios and suppliers to see how they store their glass. You may not have all the room they have, but you can use many of their storage solutions.

Lamp Forms

Lamp forms that are not being used need to be stored away from the work area. Their mass and bulk make them a real nuisance if they have to be pushed around, stepped over or constantly moved in the course of a work session. The number of available molds in different shapes and sizes compounds the need for proper storage of these unwieldy tools.

Whether the forms you own are solid or hollow, wood, fiberglass or another material, store them in a place away from the work area. A

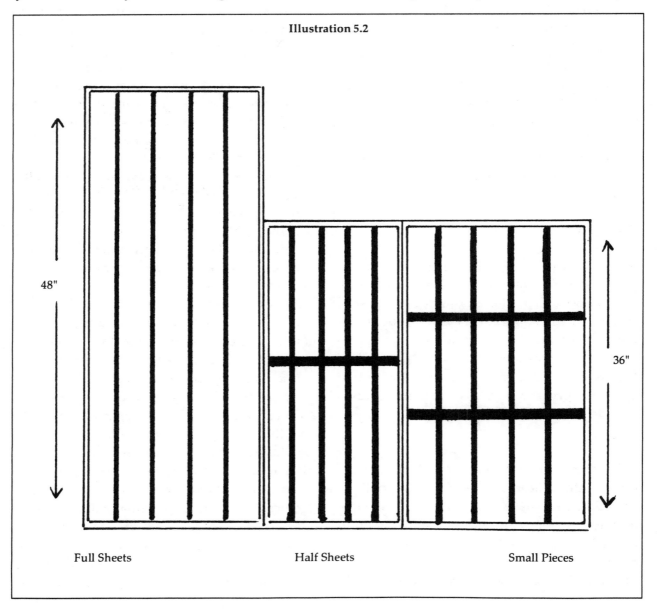

Illustration 5.2

48"

36"

Full Sheets   Half Sheets   Small Pieces

corner or designated storage area in the studio will suffice. If you are working in a home studio, a garage, attic space or utility area will do. The idea is to keep them from our immediate sphere of activity, where they will definitely be in the way.

Hollow molds stack very easily. Fiberglass molds in particular can be stacked upside down, with the largest at the bottom and smaller molds inside. Fiberglass forms can also be hung on the walls where they will be safely out of the way until needed. Drill a small hole into the bottom edge of the form and tie a loop of string or nylon wire through the hole (be careful not to drill through any design areas). The form

can then be hung from a nail. If wall space is plentiful, many molds can be stored in this way. Smaller molds can be hung inside larger ones to further maximize this excellent use of space.

One consideration that is easily forgotten is the availability and proximity of a power source. It is undesirable and hazardous to have a web of extension cords extending throughout the work place. For those processes requiring power, a single outlet source secured at a convenient location on the worktable will suffice. One of the better solutions is to secure a power strip horizontally, directly under the table top, against one of the long two-by-four stretchers. The power cord can be kept from the floor by

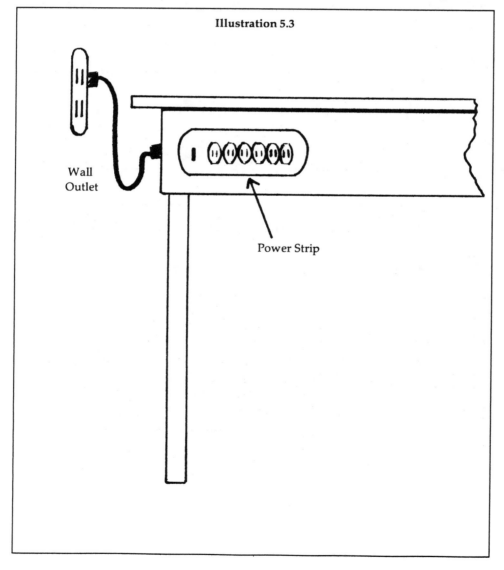

Illustration 5.3

Wall Outlet

Power Strip

positioning one end of the table against a wall where an outlet exists or has been installed (see Illus. 5.3). Multiple outlets of this type can be installed around the table as needed. Employ the services of a licensed electrician if you have any doubts about your ability in this area.

Radios, coffee makers, food, utensils, and other domestic items have no place on the work table. They should be kept safely out of reach and out of the way of work patterns. Food and drink should not be in the work place at all, for health reasons. Distractions can cause you to slip up when doing difficult tasks.

Take the time to efficiently set up and maintain your work space and your work and working attitude will profit.

Making Your Own Worktable

To build a simple worktable, you will need the following:

- Ten 2 x 4 studs
- One 4 x 8 ¼" or ½" plywood sheet
- One box each: 6D and 8D finishing nails
- Measuring tape
- Builder's square
- Circular saw
- Hammer

The worktable consists of an upper and lower rectangular frame supported by six legs. The 4x8 work surface sits atop the upper frame (see Illus. 5.4). This worktable is built to a final

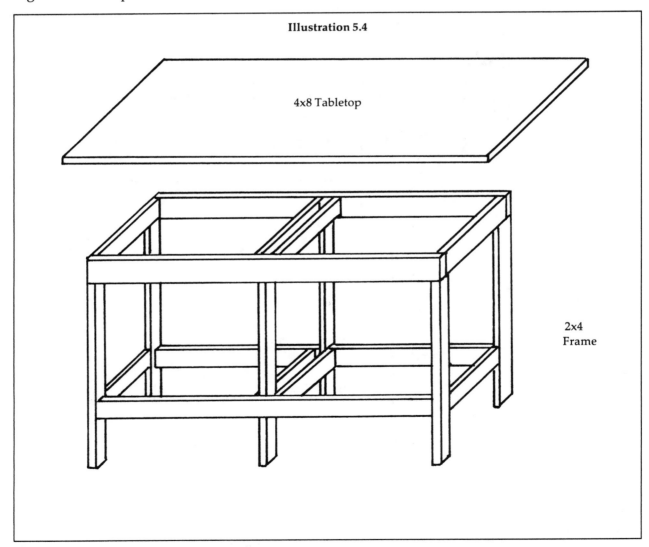

Illustration 5.4

4x8 Tabletop

2x4
Frame

height of 36". Although the height is arbitrary, 36" is usually a comfortable and convenient height whether you work sitting or standing.

To begin, cut six lengths of 2 x 4 stock, 35¾" long. These members are the six legs. Next, cut four lengths 93" long. These are the long upper and lower stretchers of the frame. Finally, you will need eight lengths, each 41" long, for the side and middle frame members.

Take two 93" and two 41" lengths and nail them into position, using a builder's square to keep the corner angles true (see Illus. 5.5). Be sure the shorter lengths are nailed inside the longer ones. Mark the center of the long stretchers with a straight line on the outside.

Four 35 ¾" lengths are now nailed into position as legs. With the large frame flat on the ground, nail the legs securely to the corners as illustrated (see Illus. 5.6). Make sure the edges of the verticals sit flat on the floor. This will make these edges flush with the top of the frame. The work surface will sit on these edges.

Position one of the remaining 2 x 4 legs along a 93" stretcher with its thin edge centered at the mark. Nail it into place. Position one of the remaining 41" lengths against it and nail it into

place. If cut accurately, it should sit inside the two opposing 93" stretchers. Nail a second 41" length on the opposite side of the vertical. Repeat this procedure on the other 93" 2 x 4. When completed, the entire structure should look like Illus. 5.7.

The remaining lengths of 2 x 4 are used to construct a second 93" by 44" support frame. These members are nailed approximately 12" from the bottom of the table legs, as shown in Illus. 5.8.

The 4' x 8' sheet of plywood is nailed to the top of the frame. Remember that the frame has been assembled upside down. (A lower shelf can be installed onto the lower frame braces, if desired. This shelf will provide added storage space. To make this, you will need an additional sheet of plywood with notches cut out to accommodate the positions of the existing legs. This should be installed prior to fastening the lower stretchers to the legs.)

A protective 4' x 8' sheet of Homasote can be laid on the tabletop if desired. Homasote is available at lumber yards and is commonly used for model railroad surfaces. It provides a softer surface than the plywood and is an excel-

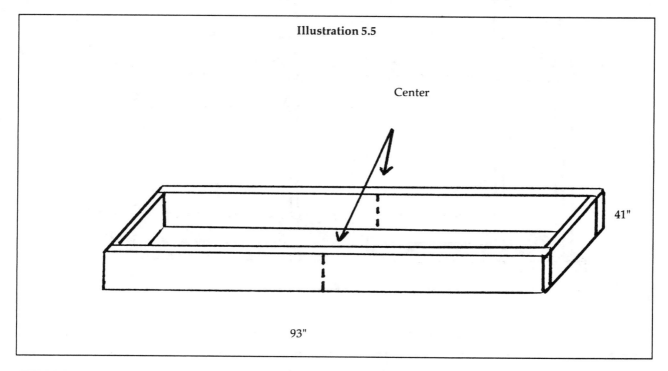

Illustration 5.5

Center

41"

93"

THE LAMPMAKING HANDBOOK

Illustration 5.7

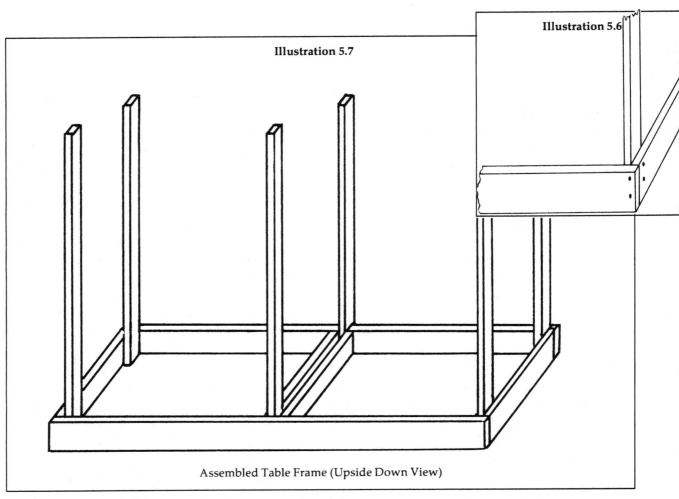

Assembled Table Frame (Upside Down View)

Illustration 5.6

Illustration 5.8

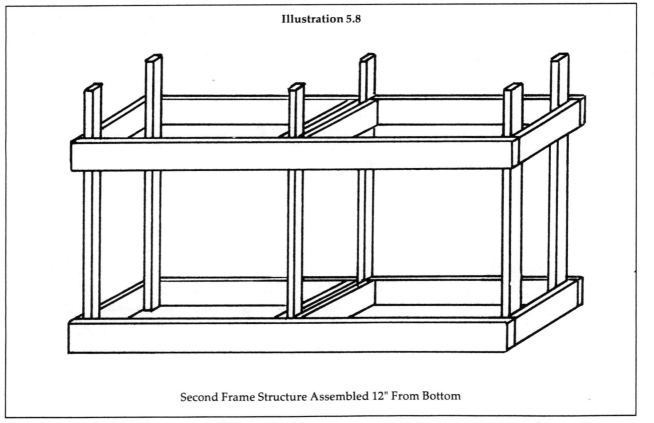

Second Frame Structure Assembled 12" From Bottom

lent cutting and working surface. It also protects the plywood from the deteriorating effects of cutting wheels, flux and other chemicals. The Homasote can easily be replaced if necessary.

If a 4' x 8' table is inconvenient for your particular work space, the methods described can be adapted to any size table. Build to suit your own work space.

Making A Light Table

The structure itself is simple. A box frame of 1 x 6 lumber supported by legs. The box is enclosed by a sheet of plywood on the bottom and a glass or Plexiglass surface on top. Lighting fixtures are secured inside.

If work space permits, the light table's surface should accommodate the largest of your lamp designs. For instance, the layout sheet of a 28" Magnolia, one of the largest of available Tiffany designs, is 22" by 32". The light table's surface should be larger. A good size is 30" by 48" by 40" high. This area will provide ample space for most lamp layouts plus the inevitable accumulation of glass pieces that always accompany a lamp project. Table height is an arbitrary matter. You should use your own judgement to determine the height at which you'll be most efficient and comfortable. Keep in mind that you will be spending a great deal of time and energy at this work station.

The same tools used in constructing the worktable are used for the light table, except that wood screws are used to secure the sides of

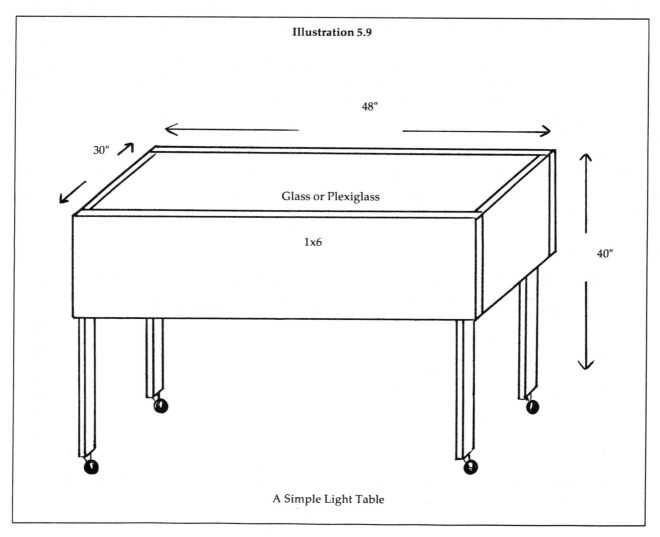

Illustration 5.9

48"

30"

Glass or Plexiglass

1x6

40"

A Simple Light Table

the box frame. To build the light table in Illus. 5.9, you will need the following materials:

- Four pieces 1 x 6, two pieces 40" long, two pieces 28 ¾"
- Four 2 x 4 studs, 39¾" long
- ¼" or ½" square molding, 15 linear feet.
- One sheet ¼" plywood cut to size, 30" x 40"
- ¼" clear plate glass or Plexiglass, 28½" x 38½"
- A box of 2" wood screws
- Three to six light sockets and bulbs

Lay out the four lengths of 1 x 6. Measure ¼" down from one edge of each piece and draw a line along the entire length. Cut the square molding strips into two 20" and two 40" lengths. Screw these lengths, the shortest onto the shorter 1 x 6s and the longer onto the longest, using ¾" to ⅞" wood screws, into position. Match the top edge of the molding along the drawn line. This will recess the molding ¼" down from the edge of the 1 x 6s. The molding strips serve as a support rail for the glass surface (see Illus. 5.10).

Using the four cut pieces of 1 x 6, build a box-like frame. Screw the sides into each other. Use a square to keep the corner angles true.

Fasten the ends of the box inside the 40" sides (see Illus. 5.11).

With the assembled box-frame sitting on the floor, measure and mark ¼" up from the bottom at each corner. Extend this mark as a line 2" long from each corner. Take one 39 ¾" 2 x 4 and position it into the corner with its widest side against the 30" wall of the frame and its end on the marked line (see Illus. 5.12). Screw it into place using 2" wood screws. Fasten it against both the long and short walls of the frame. With the structure upside down, repeat the procedure in all four corners.

To fit the 30" by 40" plywood sheet onto the bottom of the frame structure, it is necessary to make cut-outs for the table legs. Measure 2" from the edge of the longest side and 4" into the shortest side, drawing a perpendicular line from each until they meet (see Illus. 5.13). This rectangular shape can then be cut out from the sheet and nailed to the bottom edge of the light table structure. The legs will correspond to the new cut-outs. Once the plywood sheet is fastened to the bottom, the entire structure can be set upright.

To maximize the interior light of the box, the inside walls and bottom should be painted white. Lighting fixtures should be installed at

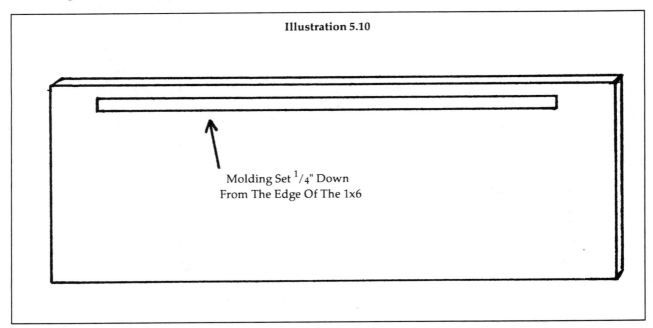

Illustration 5.10

Molding Set ¼" Down
From The Edge Of The 1x6

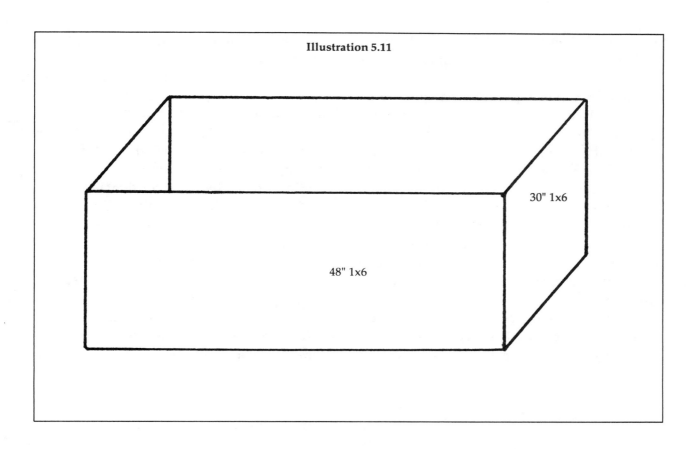

Illustration 5.11

30" 1x6

48" 1x6

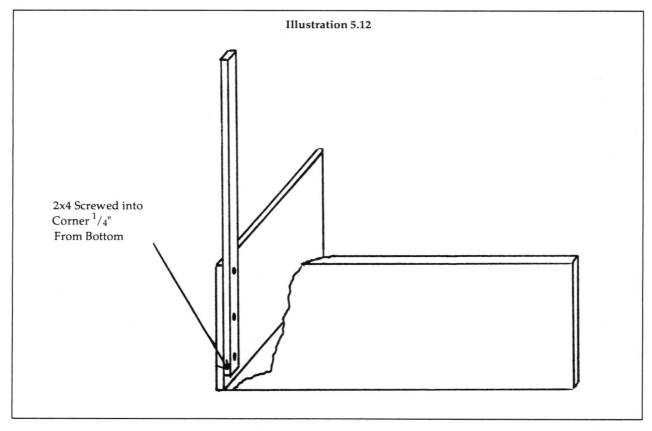

Illustration 5.12

2x4 Screwed into Corner $^1/_4$" From Bottom

this time. To simulate the lighting of the lamp, a cluster of three incandescent bulbs should be fixed to the inside of the light box. The choice of incandescent over fluorescent has to do with the effect the different kinds of light have on the glass we will be using. Fluorescent light activates colors in the glass that will not be present once the lamp is lit by incandescent bulbs. Unexpected and undesirable hues and color values will appear in the final result.

Light sockets can be secured to threaded nipples fitted through drilled holes in the bottom of the light table. Wiring should extend through the nipples and join beneath the light box, controlled by an on-off switch. You can also contain the wiring inside the box and join all connections to a dimmer switch fixed to one side of the light box with the control knob installed through a hole and extending to the exterior for easy access. A dimmer switch will offer the most versatility in simulating changes in glass color in varying degrees of light. Consult with an licensed electrician concerning if necessary.

With lighting installed and operable, the glass tabletop can be lowered into the frame. The edges of the glass will rest upon the square molding strips fastened to the light box sides.

One further embellishment to a light table is the addition of casters. Casters or wheels, available at hardware and home improvement centers can easily be installed into holes drilled under the four light table legs. Where several craftspeople share the cutting, layout or assembly, a light table that can be easily moved is very useful. A movable table can also be placed out of the way when not in use. ◾

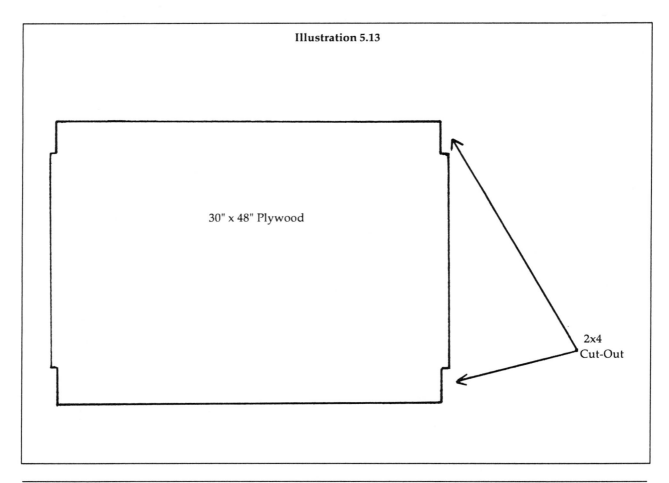

Illustration 5.13

30" x 48" Plywood

2x4 Cut-Out

6

Beginning Your Lamp

The first steps in lamp construction are cutting the glass and preparing the template. A template is a physical replica of one outlined space of the lamp design. Each space has its corresponding template. Accuracy of the template is imperative if the resulting cut pieces of glass are to fit correctly onto the mold during assembly.

With commercially available lamp molds and designs, template sheets are provided in either paper or mylar. They are usually accompanied by an identical sheet used for laying out the completed pieces of glass into their proper place. The individual pieces are outlined in black and the spaces are identified with numbers and sometimes letters distinguishing the different elements of the design (i.e., 1F=flower pattern, 6L=leaf pattern). Preparation is the same for either a mylar or a paper template.

Template outlines represent the solder lines that will ultimately join the pieces of glass. These lines become the space between the glass pieces into which the solder will flow, creating the network of metal that holds the work together. The black outlines must therefore be removed from the edges of each template to allow for this space. These outlines should be approximately $\frac{1}{16}$" wide, thus allowing the proper amount of space between pieces. Anything larger risks leaving too much space between pieces, resulting in unsightly, thick lines, a waste of solder and difficulty in assembly. If the outlines are not trimmed from the template, the resulting pieces will be too big. When assembled into place, these untrimmed pieces will extend beyond their pre-set boundaries.

Before cutting individual template pieces from the master sheet, prepare envelopes in which to save them, labeling each envelope by the type of template pieces it will hold, for example, flowers, background, stems, or other pieces. Keep these envelopes on hand as you cut your templates.

Ordinary scissors can be used to cut templates from the master sheet. The outline is removed in two consecutive steps. First, the outline is cut with the entire black line left intact. Cutting is done along its outside edge. Second, the remaining black line is carefully cut away from the template. Any sharp burrs or excess material are removed. When doing this, remember that the outer edge of the outline represents the inner edge on an adjoining template. It is very easy to inadvertently cut into the surrounding shapes. Take care that you do not damage them.

If you are using pattern shears, be aware of the thickness of the center blade. If it is more than $1/16$", as is the blade on those used for lead came work, too much material will be removed from the template. Pattern shears are available with thinner blades for copper foil work. Some expensive types have interchangeable blades for each type of cut. Nonetheless, check the width of the center blade of any pattern shears you use and cut the right size heartline. Once you cut templates too small, they cannot be made bigger; you will have to create an entirely new set. This is not a problem if only one, or a few patterns need to be made. If an entire set of patterns has been improperly prepared, however, the creation of a new set can be a mountain of undesirable work.

Cutting templates with pattern shears must be done more carefully than with conventional scissors. The pattern shears remove outline material in one pass, affecting a selected template piece and all of its surrounding shapes simultaneously. Critical accuracy is needed to avoid damaging the edges of surrounding shapes.

The most common problem with pattern shears is the buildup of waste heartline material at the joint of the three cutting blades. While most of the heartline strips will fall from the tool after being cut, some become lodged between the blades. If this material is not immediately removed from the tool, it will affect the shearing action by causing the blades to pull or crimp the material rather than cut it. This can easily damage the outline edges and the templates themselves. Take your time when using pattern shears and remove any excess pattern material from the blades as it accumulates. Proper use of pattern shears can reduce template-making time by half of that spent using conventional scissors. The little time needed to ensure accuracy and effective cutting will not be wasted.

Periodically check the accuracy of your tem-

plates against their corresponding space on the lamp mold. Simply take a prepared template and hold it against its corresponding space on the mold. If properly shaped and cut, it will occupy the space perfectly, showing only the outline drawn on the mold around its edges. If this outline cannot be seen, your template is too big and should be trimmed accordingly. If you see blank space within the outline and around the outside edges of the template, it is too small. A new, larger template needs to be made.

If you need to make a new template to replace one damaged, lost or improperly cut, follow these instructions:

1. Cut a piece of template material a little larger than what is needed.

2. Hold it against its space on the mold surface. You should be able to see the outline of the shape through the template material.

3. With a fine-tip marking pen, trace the outline onto the template material. Transfer the pattern number also.

4. Cut out the pattern as if it were the original using the guidelines given above.

Cutting Glass With A Template

Cutting glass pieces for a lamp without using templates or patterns is not advisable. Unlike flat glass projects, all of the glass pieces of a lamp need to fit into a puzzle-like configuration that interlocks around a 360-degree design. Because most designs repeat a number of times, each piece of glass must be identical in shape and detail to its counterparts. If the glass pieces are cut over a light table and through the master design sheet, as can be done with flat glass panels, it is almost impossible to guarantee such accuracy unless each piece, after being cut, is matched to its template, or against its place on the mold, then trimmed into shape accordingly.

Most craftspeople have a tendency to under, or over-cut glass when cutting without the use of a template or over a light table. Even if the amount cut over or under size is minimal, it will make a noticeable difference when assembling the lamp. Any inaccuracy in size or shape affects the surrounding pieces of glass. If they are shifted out of position by a piece that is either too big or incorrectly shaped, they will, in turn, shift other pieces out of position. This domino effect will continue throughout the entire assembly procedure until the final pieces are assembled. At this point, the inability of the last pieces of glass to fit properly will have to be addressed and corrected, usually by drastic measures. Remaining large pieces will have to be cut smaller than their proper size. On the other hand, if all of the glass pieces were cut too small, a large gap will accrue where the edges of the design should marry. Either condition is unacceptable. The most effective way to avoid such problems is to cut to your template and grind accurately.

Cutting Techniques

A proper score on glass is made by knowing how the cutter's wheel should engage the glass and what makes a good score. This knowledge will help you perfect your cutting technique.

All glass cutters, regardless of style, size or cost, are designed to have their cutting wheels meet the glass surface perpendicular to that surface. The wheel must stand at a right angle to the glass before any pressure is exerted to score the glass. The wheel must also turn freely during the score. A wheel that cannot spin or is kept from spinning during a score will merely scratch the glass surface rather than score it. This damages the surface of the glass and renders the cutting wheel useless by flawing the roundness of its edge. Such a cutting wheel cannot score properly and needs to be replaced. Keep the wheel lubricated during use by oc-

casionally dipping it into a suitable lubricant. (Many stained glass suppliers carry a pre-mixed cutting oil, or you can easily prepare one by simply mixing one-half motor oil with one-half kerosene.)

Proper cutting technique begins with holding the cutting tool. Although traditional glass cutters are designed to be held in one way only, the growing popularity of stained glass has brought about other methods of holding the cutter, and accordingly, new glass cutters designed to accommodate these variations. These techniques are acceptable if they can produce a proper score effectively and efficiently. Others, such as holding the cutter with two hands or clenching the tool in a fist, make the action more difficult and can discourage accuracy.

The photos shown here outline the traditional method of holding the glass cutter and scoring the glass. Cutting glass against templates will encourage speed and accuracy in lampmaking. The following will best promote the achievment of those goals:

Photo 6.1: Position the handle of the glass cutter between the middle and forefinger, with the base of the handle resting against the thumb, which supports the tool from behind. Many cutting tools have a recessed area at the bottom of the handle, which is for the forefinger. If the cutter has breaking teeth or notches, they should face the rear.

Photo 6.2: Place the edge of the cutting wheel against the glass, holding the tool in a perpendicular position to the glass surface. Do not exert any pressure until you are in that position. The cutting wheel must point in the direction of the score.

Photo 6.3: Score by applying pressure to the cutting tool and directing it along the surface of the glass. Always cut toward the body; cutting away from the body does not encourage proper control of the tool. It is also easy for the cutter

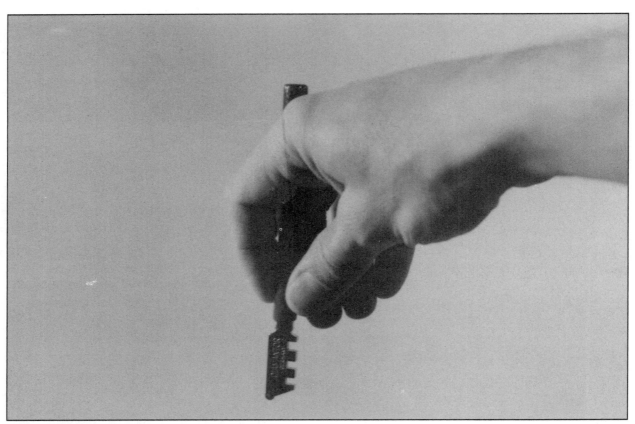

Photo 6.1: The proper way to hold a cutter.

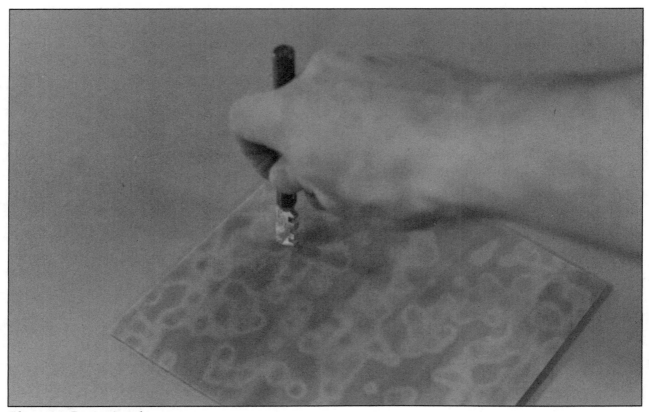

Photo 6.2: Beginning the score.

to slip forward, causing an accident. Glass should always be cut with caution, no matter how simple it seems.

Exert pressure from the entire arm and not from the wrist; it should not be excessive. By distributing this downward pressure throughout the arm, you will cut down on any feelings of stress and discomfort. Once you are comfortable with this procedure, practice your cutting until you can score a clean and even line. After a while, you will automatically apply the right amount of pressure.

Too much pressure will over-score the glass, resulting in a deep scratch rather than a score. This scratch will not produce a clean break in the glass, causing it instead to fracture away from the score, breaking unpredictably. It is also a good practice to score your individual pieces of glass from one edge of the glass sheet to the other. A continuous score across the entire surface will break out easier.

Most glasses score with a distinctive crackle, though some produce no sound. Scoring should make a visible scoreline on the glass.

Compared to other methods of holding the glass cutter, this technique allows the most control over the tool while requiring the least amount of pressure. It only occupies one hand, leaving the other free to hold the template in place. Also, a maximum amount of viewing space is left around the tool. This clearance is needed when cutting around templates.

If you hold your glass cutter differently and achieve satisfactory results doing so, continue. In the end, you are striving for speed and accuracy in your glass cutting. Any technique that delivers that result is valid. But do try this technique. You may find it improves your performance and saves time and energy. Now on to cutting our glass pieces.

Cutting The Glass

Photo 6.4: Isolate the template on a piece of glass that is slightly larger than the template.

Hold the template with your free hand and score along one complete side, beginning and ending the score at opposite edges of the glass. Without moving the template out of position, turn both it and the glass to the next edge to be scored. Make sure the template is lined up with the previous score line before going any further. Score the next edge in the same way. Continue doing so until all sides of the template have been scored.

The wheel of your glass cutter should ride along the template's edge. With practice, you should be able to guide your cutter along its perimeter without it wandering away from, or cutting into the template. Take your time and practice. Time spent perfecting your cutting technique translates into time saved in actual lamp production.

Straight lines are scored by pulling the cutter along the glass toward the body. Curves are cut by turning the entire tool in the direction of the curve, avoiding scraping the wheel sideways against the glass. Inside curves are cut by first scoring along the edge of the template, then making a series of "safety cuts" out to the edge of the glass. Safety cuts are successive, arc-shaped scores that allow you to work your way into the deep inside curve by breaking the glass, arc by arc, into the curve.

Photo 6.5: You can either break the glass out as it is scored or wait until the entire shape and all edges have been scored, breaking all the pieces out in succession. Whichever you choose, break the glass with a tool designated as a glass breaker, not a glass grozer. A glass breaker does not have any ridged surfaces on the inside of its jaws. It has two smooth surfaces which grasp the glass securely and permit a clean break.

Hold the glass piece in one hand and secure the jaws of the breaker against the scoreline without covering it. A slight upward and outward separating movement should facilitate the break along the scoreline. Continue around the outline of the glass shape until all breaks

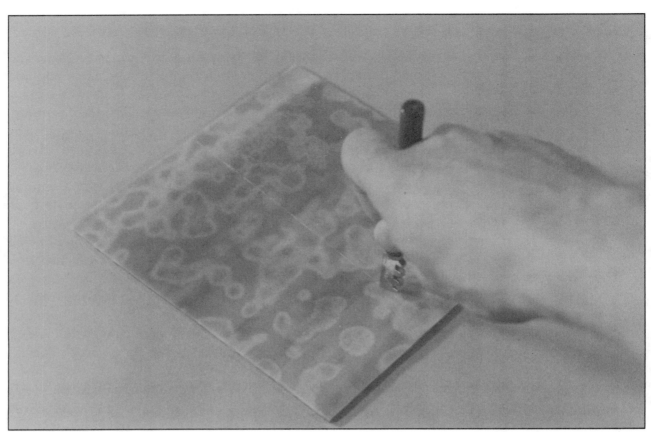

Photo 6.3: A straight and sure scoreline.

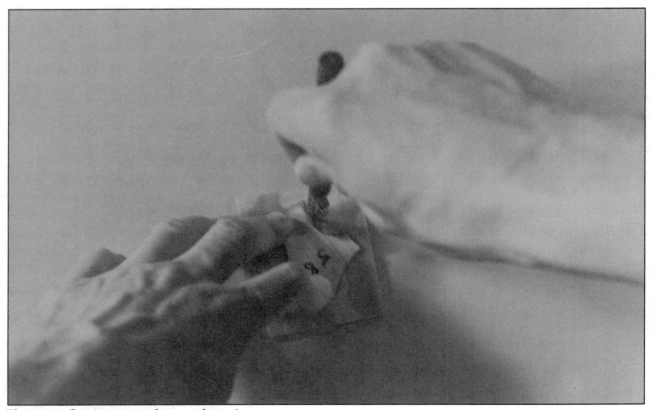

Photo 6.4: Cutting around a template piece.

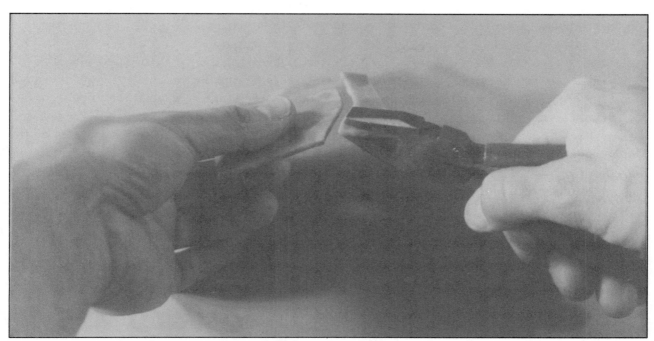

Photo 6.5: A clean break along a curving scoreline.

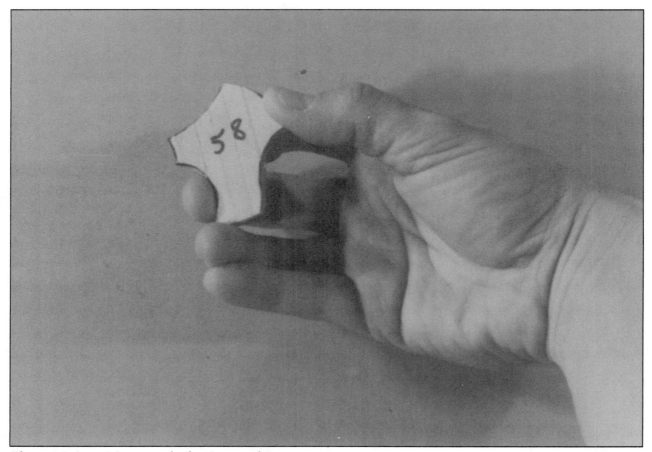

Photo 6.6: A cut piece matched to its template.

have been made and the shape is freed from its surrounding glass. Once complete, check the glass piece against its template.

A piece carefully cut and checked against the pattern will need little fine tuning at the grinder. If more shaping is necessary, do it before assembly. Simply checking the glass piece against its template while grinding will ensure accuracy. Accuracy is essential if the glass pieces are to assemble on the mold without extensive modification(see Photo 6.6).

When scoring a number of similar pieces from one template, score all pieces of glass before breaking them out. By doing this, you will save time picking up and putting down your glass cutter and breaker. It may not seem like much at first, but if you multiply the few seconds saved between these movements by the total number of pieces that need to be cut for the lamp, it can represent much time. This technique is most effective when cutting multiples of geometric glass pieces. ■

7

Lamp Construction

Copper foiling is the technique of wrapping glass pieces in thin metal foil, and it can be traced to the earliest days of lampmaking. Lead came was too cumbersome to assume the small and intricate shapes employed in lamp designs. Something extremely flexible and more conducive to thin and graceful lines was needed, specifically for lamp design and fabrication. Early experiments used a lead milled paper thin and wrapped around the glass, but the lead quickly melted from the heat of the soldering iron. The use of copper, a metal with a much higher melting point than lead, was an innovation allegedly pioneered by the Tiffany Studios (adding to the many contributions they made to art glass manufacturing and technique). Copper foil provided the glass pieces with a very thin frame of metal onto which solder could be applied to secure or "tack" one piece of wrapped glass to another. This was true in both a flat glass application, such as a panel, and in dimensional projects, such as leaded lamps. Copper foil also allowed the glass to be soldered to metals of higher integrity, such as bronze, brass and copper.

Early lampmakers had to cut, or slice their strips of foil from a large sheet and use an applied adhesive to secure the copper foil around the perimeter of the glass. This adhesive was commonly a beeswax mixture brushed onto the rear of the foil like a paste. This temporary adhesive was needed to keep the foil from moving or falling off the edge of the glass during wrapping, keeping it stationary until the glass pieces could be soldered into place.

The beeswax was successful for the most part. Unfortunately, where conditions caused the wax to harden or be disturbed, it would eventually crumble and fall out. It is not uncommon to find old lamps in which the glass, no longer secured against the inner surface of the foil by the wax, rattles so freely inside its copper foil that it appears adhesive was never present.

The wax itself had to be applied to the back of the foil in the studio. Not so today. Copper foil is now available in a number of fractional sizes and colored backings for various kinds of applications. All are prepared with a state-of-the-art adhesive backing protected by a backing tape. The backing tape is peeled away during the wrapping procedure.

The most commonly used widths of copper

foil for lampmaking are those listed below:

- ⁵⁄₃₂": For thinner types of glass.

- ³⁄₁₆": The most widely used size, it will accommodate a wide variety of flat glasses and some textured glasses of low profile.

- ⁷⁄₃₂": A wide foil used primarily for flat glasses of unusual thickness and textured glass that cannot be properly foiled with a thinner strip. It will also work on less dramatic drapery glasses.

- ¼": Used for high profile textured glass and drapery glass.

Today's copper foils are available in three thicknesses, 1 mil., 1.5 mil. and 3 mil. The thinnest of the foils is the most flexible, wrapping around the glass with the greatest ease. Because they are so soft, it is possible to crimp thinner foils around the edges of the glass without first protecting the tips of your fingers. Not so with 1.5 and 3 mil. foils. Thinner foils break or tear if, during wrapping, they encounter a sharp edge (usually when being wrapped around a corner). Use your own judgement as to which thickness of foil will suit your purposes. It's a good general practice to keep three widths of copper foil on hand when wrapping glass pieces. In most situations ⁵⁄₃₂", ³⁄₁₆" and ⁷⁄₃₂" foil will accommodate the various thicknesses of most glass pieces. (These three sizes were kept on hand for the 18" Rose Border lamp.) A copper foil dispenser is useful to hold a number of rolls at the ready.

Remember, the copper foil wrapped around the glass pieces provides a metal surface to which similarly prepared glass pieces can be permanently tacked and soldered. The solder forms the network of metal holding the artwork together, forming a veritable skeleton of lead/tin alloy enclosing each piece of glass by its edges and fusing it to its neighboring pieces.

Copper is conducive to accepting molten solder onto its surface. Copper's high melting point allows the re-working and constant re-application of intense heat and solder without damaging the material. When free of any oxidation or dirt, and prepared with an appropriate flux, copper foil efficiently provides the permanent metal-to-metal adhesion that is required in lampmaking.

Proper foiling techniques guarantee the material's efficiency. Regardless of a glass' thickness, all pieces need to be wrapped and prepared with copper foil in the same way. The edges of the glass must be covered and a small lip or overhang of foil needs to extend onto the front and rear surfaces. This extending foil is then crimped against the glass.

The amount of foil folded over the glass should be carefully considered. Too much foil extending onto the surfaces of glass will only add to the finished size of the surface lead line, providing a wider surface over which heat can react upon the glass. Heat cracks and checking (hairline fissures on either or both surfaces of the glass) can occur.

On the other hand, too little copper foil will fail to secure the glass in its place. To some, super thin lead lines are considered a sign of technical perfection. In reality, they deprive a leaded shade of strength. Granted, fat, lumpy and irregular leading does very little for the visual appeal of a traditionally crafted shade. On the other hand, weakening the structure for the sake of vanity is a high price to pay and does nothing for the cause of fine lampmaking. A happy medium is best.

As the diameter of a lamp increases, the amount of stress the soldered network of metal must bear also increases. Larger lamps obviously accrue more weight in glass and solder than smaller ones. This weight, as it is distributed over the curve of the shade, provides constant tension on the lead lines. Add to this the cumulative buildup of heat from the lighting source inside a lamp. If lead lines are too thin, a gradual softening can occur. As the solder softens from the constant heat, the downward weight of the shade will cause the metal framework to stretch. Copper foil will be pulled from the edge of the glass. Small specks of escaping light will be evident where this occurs. If the condition is not checked and corrected, it will be followed by a loosening of the glass pieces themselves. The foil will continue to separate from the glass. This condition will proliferate where the heat buildup is the greatest, around the aperture of the shade.

The greater part of this stress can be countered by allowing a small amount of space between individual pieces of glass (established by the heartline removed from the glass templates) into which the molten solder can fall during soldering. Also wrap a sufficient amount of foil onto the surface of the glass. This amount can vary in proportion to the size of the shade. Small shades (20" or less in diameter) enjoy a very strong skeletal structure of solder lines and reinforcing materials (aperture and bottom rings). Wrapping $1/16$" of foil over the surfaces of the glass will suffice. Where many tiny pieces of glass are incorporated into the design, the amount of foil can be reduced to a minimal $1/32$".

Glass pieces for larger shades can be wrapped using the same $1/16$" guideline, provided the design is a relatively busy one and the individual pieces of glass are not too big. If they are big, you will want to increase the amount of overlapping foil to approximately $3/32$". These increases are accomplished by switching to a wider foil, $3/16$" or $7/32$", for example.

A good rule of thumb is to keep an equal amount of foil wrapped onto the front and back surfaces of the glass. This will allow the solder to effectively grasp the piece of glass around its entire perimeter.

Textured glasses, ripples and draperies, require special handling. The copper foil must grasp the edges of this glass the same way it does flat glass, but the surface irregularities add varying amounts of mass to the width of the glass. A wider foil should be used to properly wrap these glasses.

The best support will be provided on textured glass if the foil covers all of the surface edges, no matter how high or irregularly shaped they may be. In some cases, especially when wrapping high-profile drapery glasses, a single width of foil, even a very wide $1/4$" foil will not suffice. In these cases "double" foiling is necessary. Double foiling is simply using two strips of foil to create one very wide single strip (refer to Illus. 4.10).

Copper foiling can be a major investment of time in the scope of the entire project, according to how many pieces need to be foiled. There's no getting away from it. To expedite this stage in your project, I suggest the following:

1. Have enough of the required sizes of copper foil on hand. Substitutions will provide inadequate results. And time lost to last minute shopping for supplies is time lost, period!

2. Don't advance to wrapping until all of the glass is cut and ground. If it is practical to lay the entire lamp out, do so before you begin foiling.

3. Do not foil, then stop to crimp the foil around the edges. This stop-and-start action just wastes time. Foil all the pieces, then return and crimp them.

4. Protect the tips of your fingers with some kind of thimble-like covering. Masking tape wrapped around the pads of your fingertips provides a semi-hard surface.

5. Use a fid, or crimping device, only if you feel it is absolutely necessary. The habitual use of a fid, whether the foil needs further crimping or not, can waste valuable assembly time.

6. If it is impractical to have all of the lamp's pieces laid out on the design, keep background, flower, leaf, stem, and border pieces separate. Place them in individual, plastic food storage bags. Once they're foiled, this will make laying them out much easier.

Assembly

The lamp pieces are cut. They have been ground to shape, wrapped with foil and laid out on the master design sheet (see photo 7.1). You can now begin assembling the glass design directly onto the mold.

Position yourself with your soldering equipment on your right side (or left, if you are left-handed) the lamp mold in front of you and the layout of glass pieces on your opposite side.

You should set one of two types of brass fixtures into the aperture at the top of the mold, onto which you can begin tacking the glass pieces. Use either a brass cap that has been fixed to the aperture by a threaded nipple secured through a drilled hole in the top of the mold, or a Tiffany-type aperture ring set into a recess molded into the top of the lamp form. The 18" Rose Border lamp utilizes the latter.

When soldering copper foiled pieces against a metal surface, such as a brass aperture ring or cap, be aware of how these metals react to the application of heat, flux and solder. Because brass does not have the conductivity of copper, and because rings and caps have greater mass than the thin strips of copper foil, more heat will be required for these metals to accept the solder.

To achieve the proper bond, flux the metal part to be soldered (including the wrapped glass piece), with a water-based or paste flux. Apply heat with the soldering iron directly to the metal ring or cap at the point where it is to join with the foiled piece of glass. When the metal is heated to the correct temperature, it will actually "grab" the solder in a quick, absorbing motion. As the solder liquifies (it be-comes thinner and freer-flowing as it becomes hotter) extend it onto the glass piece by dragging the soldering iron over the edge receiving the tack. This is called "sweating" solder onto the metal and is a technique frequently used in lampmaking, as well as glass craft in general.

The design of the lamp should be clearly visible. Beginning with a piece of glass from the top left of the lamp, place it in position on the mold and tack solder it into place against the aperture hardware (see photo 7.2). If the templates were carefully cut and are true to their corresponding outlines on the mold design, and if the glass was properly cut to these patterns, the wrapped pieces should fit inside the outlines drawn on the mold. The outline should be visible around the perimeter of the piece once it has been placed in position. If they are placed in this way, a small amount of space should surround every piece. This space, originally occupied by the heartline removed when the templates were cut, will allow solder to reach in between the pieces of glass and form a strong, supporting metal network.

Follow this assembly procedure with the next piece, and continue around the top of the lamp, applying a small amount of flux and tacking each piece to the cap or ring as you go (see photo 7.3). You will be immediately aware of any inaccuracies in the size of the glass pieces. If they are too small, they will "swim" inside their appropriate positions; excessive space will surround them. If they are too big, they will crowd the other pieces out of position.

Any inaccuracies that appear must be addressed now, as they occur. Assembling the lamp in a continuing downward spiral allows these corrections to be made immediately instead of at the end of assembly, when the conditions are most difficult to correct.

If a glass piece is too small, you can spread its adjoining pieces farther apart. This technique will eat up excessive space around the glass pieces. Just a slight spreading of each piece will effectively and inconspicuously close up any

Photo 7.1: The cut pieces for the first third of the lamp, foiled and laid out .

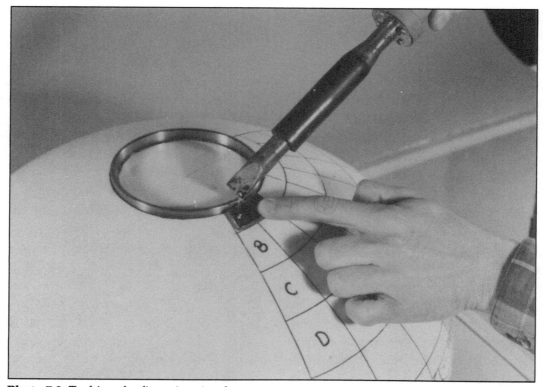

Photo 7.2: Tacking the first piece in place.

extra space by distributing it among a number of pieces. If all pieces of the lamp are too small, check your templates. They will probably also be too small, and need to be corrected. The only way to close up space on a lamp whose pieces are all cut too small is to attempt positioning the pieces a bit higher up the mold. By tacking them around a spiral of decreased perimeter, some extra space will be eliminated. Be aware that this adjustment in positioning the pieces may have to be carried out throughout the entire assembly procedure. If, after assembling a number of pieces, you find that they are tightening up or seem to crowd each other, gradually lower their positions while tacking, until they are again aligned properly.

If pieces seem too big, the copper foil must be removed and the pieces trimmed or ground to proper size. If this needs to be done only occasionally, cut down when necessary. If all pieces seem too big, again, check your templates and make any corrections. To assemble a lamp whose pieces all seem to be big, try lowering their position in relation to their space on the mold design. Assembling them around a spiral of increased diameter will provide extra space for them to fit into. Again, be aware that this procedure may have to be carried out throughout assembly unless the condition is corrected. If your design extends to the very bottom of the mold's surface, the lowest edge of the entire bottom row may need to be ground down where the glass pieces extend beyond their lowest boundary.

The above adjustments will not have to be made if you adhered to a strict policy of checking and double checking your accuracy when creating the templates and cutting the glass.

If the design incorporates a straight bottom border, the precision with which the glass pieces are assembled depends entirely upon how carefully they are set against any horizontal guidelines drawn onto the mold. To insure an aesthetically pleasing and truly straight bottom border, take your time placing these final glass pieces. If any adjustments need to be made to the pieces, make them as they are assembled onto the mold. Because the metal reinforcing ring will be applied directly to these pieces, it will reflect any waves or improper alignment in the bottom row of glass. Once the lamp is placed on a base, any waviness will be apparent.

With all the pieces tack-soldered onto the mold, the entire shade can be filled in with solder (see photo 7.4). Starting at the aperture row, fill in the area between the aperture ring or cap and the first row of glass (see photo 7.5). Continue down and around the shade until the entire lamp is done.

It is not necessary to concern yourself with the aesthetics of fine soldering at this point. Just pass the soldering iron over the lead lines, feeding just enough solder into the lead lines to fill them to the surface. Don't worry if the lines are sloppy, lumpy or otherwise unsightly. All of these conditions will be rectified during the final soldering of the lamp. The purpose of filling in the lamp with solder is simply to reinforce the structure, so that you can safely remove it from the mold.

Once this filling-in is complete, grasp the shade from its bottom edge and gently lift. If you feel resistance, tug one side of the lamp and then the other, moving around the bottom edge as you do so. If the shade still resists being removed, turn the entire unit, mold and shade, upside down and pull the mold from the inside of the lamp.

Having removed the shade from its mold, place the shade upside down on the worktable. Do not rest the lamp on its bottom edge; it is still quite vulnerable and can easily be damaged.

Exceptions

Some lamp designs present special assembly problems. The Tiffany Peony, Nasturtium and Drop Head Dragonfly forms have a double curve outline. The bottom edge of the shape curves inward, creating an edge that is of a

22"Tulip, on bronze Chinese Urn base, 1991. →

12" Geometric Lamp, 1979.

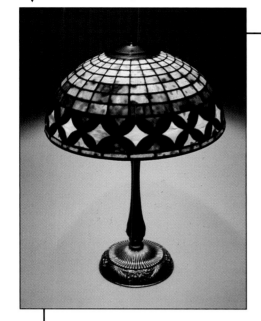

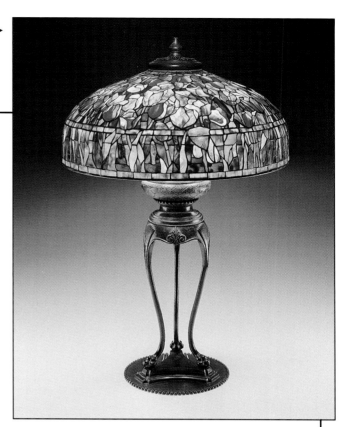

↑ 18" Wisteria, on tree trunk base. 1989.

← 20" Bouquet Lamp, 1985.

← The Other Wife, 1989

Sails On Red, 1986

↑ Landscape Through Large Windows, 1986.

← Murnau 1909, 1986.

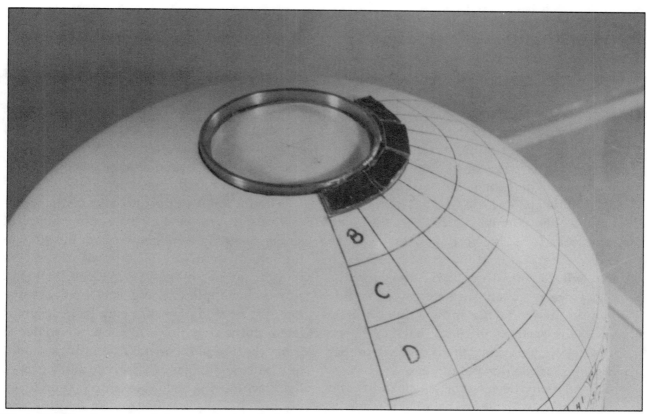

Photo 7.3: The first row of pieces tacked to the brass aperture ring.

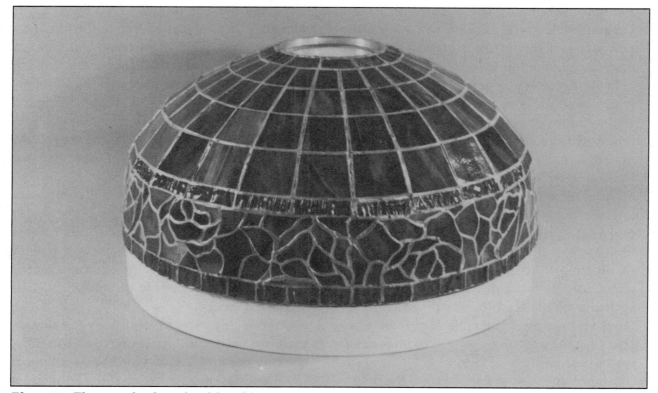

Photo 7.4: The completely tack soldered lamp.

smaller diameter than the widest section of the mold. A special technique is used to remove the assembled glass from the mold once it has been filled with solder.

As the glass is assembled onto the mold, a section of pieces extending in a vertical line from the widest point of the mold down to the bottom edge is left without being tacked together. This is done at about six locations around the shade. When filling in the lamp with solder, these spaces are again left unattached. To remove the assembled glass from the mold, gently spread the glass sections away from the mold (the vertical lead lines that weren't soldered will allow this) and lift the glass from the mold. Once removed, turn the shade upside down on the worktable and gently add pressure to the sections of glass that have been spread apart, returning them to their proper positions. Tack solder and fill these areas.

Other Tiffany designs for which forms and templates are available have similar treatments to their bottom rows but do not call for the same assembly techniques. These are the 16" Tiffany Dragonfly, Poppy, Geranium and a few others whose last geometric row of glass turns sharply inward from the row directly above.

These last rows of glass are not assembled while the shade is on the mold, but are instead soldered into position once the lamp has been removed from the form. They are held at an inward angle and set into place one at a time. Each successive piece is tilted to meet the angle of the preceding piece.

Reinforcement

Reinforcing a shade involves adding metal wires, usually brass or copper, to the skeletal structure of the lead lines, strengthening the lamp at its most vulnerable locations. These areas are the aperture opening (which has already been addressed in our procedure), the contour dome of larger shades and the bottom edge, or border.

Many shades suffer from a lack of reinforcement. Over time, heat buildup within the shade and the tensile stress the lead lines constantly endure may cause damage. Any structural weakness, especially at its bottom edge, leaves the lamp defenseless against accidental injuries in the studio, during shipping or when installed in its final location. Often, it is simply a lack of knowledge, not a production decision, to preclude proper reinforcement.

With the lamp set upside down on the worktable, use your iron to melt away any lumps of solder that may have gathered on the edge of the bottom row of glass. Lumps will prevent the reinforcing ring, in this case made of 5/32" brass, from being applied. Using steel wool, remove any dirt or oxidation that may have accumulated on the ring; this will allow the solder to properly fuse to the metal (these rings should be a bit larger than is necessary to allow proper fit). Place the ring inside the lamp as shown (see photo 7.6). Take one free end of the ring and tack solder it to the bottom border of glass by first gathering a bit of solder onto the iron's tip then applying the loaded iron to the top of the ring (see photo 7.7). As the metal becomes hot, the solder will be absorbed around the ring and sweat down, fusing with the existing lead lines of the lamp. When you see this happen, remove the iron. Be sure you tack the ring onto a line of solder and not merely onto the copper foil. All tacking of the ring to the lamp's edge must be a solder-to-solder bond.

Holding the ring on the edge of the lamp, tack it to existing lead lines every 2" to 3" all the way around the perimeter (see photo 7.8). Be sure that the ring is positioned directly on top of the glass and not slightly behind or in front. Stop about 6" from the opposite end of the ring (site of the first tack).

Remove any excess metal from the ring by grasping both ends as shown and carefully severing the metal with a hacksaw (see photo 7.9). In some cases, a heavy duty wire cutter may work.

Photo 7.5: Filling in the solder between the brass ring and first row of glass.

Photo 7.6: The shade removed from the mold and ready for interior soldering.

Photo 7.7: Tacking the end of the brass reinforcement ring to the bottom edge of the shade.

Photo 7.8: Sweating the brass reinforcement ring to several points along the perimeter of the bottom border.

Photo 7.9: Using a hacksaw to cut the end of the brass reinforcement ring to match the beginning.

Photo 7.10: Tacking the end of the brass ring into place while holding it with pliers.

Butt the ends of the ring, filing the loose edge if necessary. Hold the loose end in position by grasping it with pliers; tack-solder it against the other edge, being careful not to soften the solder joint securing the opposite end (see photo 7.10).

Once the ring is tacked onto the bottom row of glass, solder the entire ring to the bottom border. This is accomplished by applying heat and solder to the ring and letting the solder flow down to the copper foil on the edge of the glass (see photo 7.11).

Lamps with irregularly shaped bottom borders are fit with a flexible wire against the glass. The procedure is as follows:

1. Cut a piece of 14- or 16-gauge brass or copper wire. It should be longer than you need to extend around the entire bottom border. Hold one end onto the edge of the glass, over an existing solder line and tack solder it into place. Follow the edge of the glass and, carefully bending the wire around the glass, solder it to every lead line it encounters. Do not skip lead lines during this procedure. Get as complete a bond as possible to facilitate the bending of the wire as you go along. Again, be sure you get a solder-to-solder bond with each successive tack.

2. When the tacking is complete and you have returned to the starting point, sever the edge of the wire with a wire cutter and join the two edges of the wire with solder. The best joint is one that cannot be detected. A small bead of solder will cover the point where the ends meet.

3. Fill the wire-to-copper foil joint with solder. Continue until no spaces between wire and foiled edge are apparent. This will involve tilting the lamp to facilitate the

Photo 7.11: Filling in the bond between the brass ring and the bottom row of glass prior to filling in the gap between the ring ends.

downward flow of solder as it envelops the wire and copper foil. It is best accomplished by holding the lamp by its aperture opening and tilting as necessary.

Interior reinforcement of lamps 22" in diameter or larger is accomplished using the same 14- or 16-gauge brass or copper wire as on an irregular edge. The wire is soldered to existing interior lead lines, extending from the aperture of the lamp, down along the lead lines vertically, to the bottom edge. In some special cases, specifically the Tiffany Wisteria and Laburnum, additional interior reinforcement was applied. This was a wire soldered approximately one inch up from the bottom of the shade, running horizontally around the perimeter. All interior reinforcement is best left until after finish soldering.

The proper number of reinforcement wires can be determined by the number of design repeats in the shade (three repeats call for three interior reinforcement wires, etc.). Use your judgement to determine whether additional reinforcement is necessary. The installation of such will make a noticeable difference in the strength of the work. ∎

This page intentionally left blank

8

Finish Work

With assembly and reinforcing completed, the final step before patina is finish work, which begins with finish soldering. During this phase the lead lines are reworked to be consistently neat and smooth. Many beautifully colored and expertly assembled lamps suffer from poor finish soldering, apparent in lumpy lead lines and joints that are not properly fused. Fine soldering is not difficult, although it does take practice. More than anything else, it requires on the part of the craftsperson an instinctive feel for how hot the iron is and how quickly it heats the solder. This "feel" will dictate how quickly the solder can be fed into the heartlines. The more soldering a craftsperson does, the sooner this instinct develops.

The goal in fine solder work is a perfect bead. A perfect bead is simply a smooth, well-formed and consistent mound of solder, free of lumps, creases and pinholes (see Illus. 8.1).

The best bead should cover all of the copper foil on both surfaces of the glass, be consistent in height throughout the surface of the shade and be properly fused to any supplemental metal work or decoration, such as reinforcement hardware or applied filigree. Although the lead lines on the interior of the shade should be neat and consistent, interior leading does not demand the acute attention the exterior does. A low-profile bead will suffice in the interior. This can usually be accomplished with one careful pass of the iron.

To prepare for finish soldering, place the lamp upside down in front of you on your workbench. Place the iron in its caddy, flux and a flux brush to the immediate side of the lamp. Place rolls of solder on the opposite side. A short block of wood will come in handy to prop up the lamp during this procedure. Remember, the surface of the lamp to be soldered, or leaded, must always be level. This allows the molten solder to puddle in place without running off and down the glass. Puddling is the buildup of molten solder on a short expanse of lead line. The intense heat keeps the entire line molten at once. If enough solder is allowed to build up (a puddle of solder), it will form a satisfactory bead on its own and remain that way as it cools. You can then move on to the next section, repeating the same puddling technique. Puddling is most effective when soldering a tight complex of short, connected lead lines. Rather than slowly drawing the iron through every line, the entire section is heated at once with a waving motion of the iron. When practicing this technique, carefully gauge the amount of heat applied. If too much heat is allowed to build up, the solder will become too thin and fall right through the lead line without beading up at all. As soon as you see the solder puddle, remove the soldering iron and allow the metal to cool.

The following photographs illustrate finish soldering of our 18" Rose Border, and the proper positioning of the shade during this:

Photo 8.1: With the shade upside down, the interior of the aperture cap or reinforcement ring is finish soldered first. Here, a Tiffany-style 4" brass ring has been set into the opening. Apply a coating of flux to the space between the ring and the first row of glass pieces. The tip of the soldering iron is passed along the perimeter of the ring, filling the gap between it and the first row of glass with solder. The desired bead in this case is a slope of solder. Remember, that

heavier metals absorb and conduct heat much more slowly than copper foil. The soldering iron must first be applied to the heavier metal, raising its temperature first so that it will successfully receive the solder and make the bond sure. The solder can then be extended to the copper foil and the bead completed.

Photo 8.2: Tilt the lamp so that the first rows of glass are relatively flat or level with the table-top. To do this, place a thin, short piece of wood beneath the far end of the aperture opening. Flux the area and bead the section that lays flat. Stop when you see the solder flowing down or dripping in any direction. It is then necessary to shift the position of the shade until the next section to be soldered is flat. Continue around the interior until you return to the first section.

Photo 8.3: Tilt the lamp to a higher angle using a thicker piece of wood, or position the lamp between the edge of the table and your lap. Your lap provides great versatility during fin-

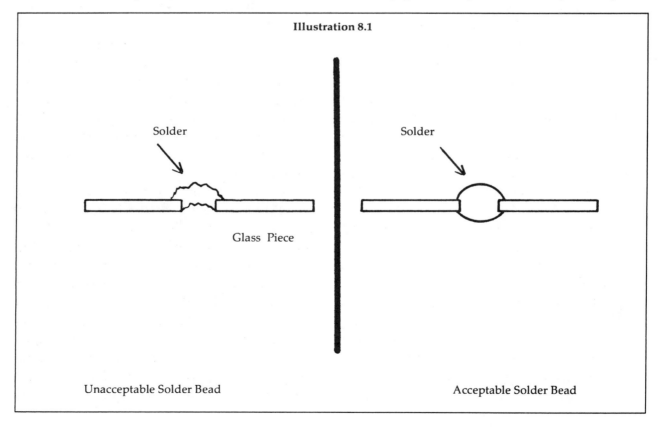

Illustration 8.1

Solder

Glass Piece

Solder

Unacceptable Solder Bead

Acceptable Solder Bead

Photo 8.1:

Photo 8.2:

ish soldering, as slight movements of either leg can alter the position of the lamp. Protect your clothing during this procedure. A heavy shop apron will provide protection from flux on the surface of the lamp and the heat that is generated by the solder. The apron should be wide enough to cover both knees. It should be washable, so that buildup of flux and dirt can be easily removed.

Continue soldering in a spiral around the whole interior. Do not attempt to finish solder the reinforcement ring attached to the bottom edge at this time; a separate technique will be discussed to accomplish this. Having completed the inside of the shade, let it cool. Use paper towels to wipe it free of excess flux and scraps of solder.

Photo 8.4: You can now finish solder the exterior. Turn the lamp right-side-up and prop it up with a wood block, as you did during the interior soldering. You may also prop the lamp on your lap and against the workbench. This allows for the most versatility when repositioning the shade from one section to the next.

The first area to solder is the joint between the aperture ring and the first row of pieces. Unlike the soldering of the interior, the exterior solder should disguise the juncture of the brass and glass, with a smooth bead of puddled solder.

Brush the entire ring and the first row of glass with flux. Apply the iron, soldering directly onto the brass ring. When the ring heats to the point that it accepts the solder (you will see it actually absorb the solder) move the iron and solder around the ring. The solder will first fuse to the brass and then travel onto the copper foiled glass. You are looking for a smooth consistent bead; if you allow too much heat to build up in one section, the solder will become too thin and flow right through the juncture. If that happens, return to that section later, after the solder has cooled, and repeat the procedure.

Photo 8.4 shows how to position the iron while feeding the solder into the joint between the ring and the shade. It also shows what the resulting bead of solder should look like. Because a cap will be seated upon this finished ring, don't build up a high mound of solder in this area. A flat bead free of pits and lumps, completely covering the ring and first row of glass, will suffice.

Continue with this technique until you reach your starting point. To successfully fuse the beginning and end points, you must reheat the entire area where the two meet. This will soften the solder enough that it will melt into, and fuse with the completed bead at the starting point.

Photo 8.5: Beginning at the top row of the shade, continue in a spiral around and down the lamp's surface, carefully fluxing and beading all of the lead lines. Go as slowly as is necessary to achieve a smooth and consistent solder line. Speed comes with practice; the objective is a fine bead.

Feed solder to the tip of the iron and to the lead line only as it's needed. A small amount of solder will go a long way given the size of most solder lines. Too much solder will be hard to control and may cause overheating of the lead lines, which will make the solder run through to the underside of the work.

As one section is completed, reposition the shade. Remember that all areas to be soldered must be flat for the solder to puddle. Working the solder at an angle is problematic; gravity will cause it to run down the shade.

When joining a new solder line to an existing one, place the tip of the iron onto the end of the existing line at the point from which the new line will extend. Apply heat until you see the end of the existing line liquify. Draw your iron away from the line, adding new solder as is necessary and continue the bead.

Photo 8.6: As you approach the edge of the lamp, it will have to be placed in position perpendicular to the work surface to facilitate beading the skirt. This is best accomplished by

Photo 8.3:

Photo 8.4:

spreading your knees and lowering the lamp between them. Do not position the lamp too high as it will be difficult to effectively view the area being soldered.

Photo 8.7: The last section of the lamp to be finish soldered is the bottom edge. With the shade upside down on the work table, the ring (which has been fixed to the edge as described in Chapter Seven) will be given a finish bead by sweating solder down onto the edge of the copper foiled pieces. This technique, more than any other, requires careful monitoring.

Begin by choosing an area away from the joint of the ring ends, thus avoiding any accidental separating of the ends by reheating. Apply flux along a short distance of the ring. Add solder to the tip of the iron and place the iron onto the top of the ring. As the metal heats up, you will see the solder being absorbed and, almost immediately, it will travel down the front of the ring until it meets the edge of the copper foiled glass. At this point, remove the iron from the area. If enough solder was applied, the resulting bead should resemble that in the photo. If the contour of the ring is still visible and the bead is not smooth, you can repeat the process once the area has cooled. If the bead is satisfactory, continue around the ring using the same technique.

Usually, sweating delivers a satisfactory bead on both the outside and inside of the bottom ring. If, upon completion, you find that areas of the inside did not bead properly, you can doctor those points by repeating the same technique with one difference. Instead of applying the heat and solder from the outside of the lamp, apply it to the inside. This will, in most cases, leave the bead on the outside intact.

To hide the seam between the two ends of the ring, carefully add solder where they meet until the joint soaks up the solder and covers the seam completely. If the solder creates an objectionable mound, apply more heat to further

Photo 8.5:

Photo 8.6:

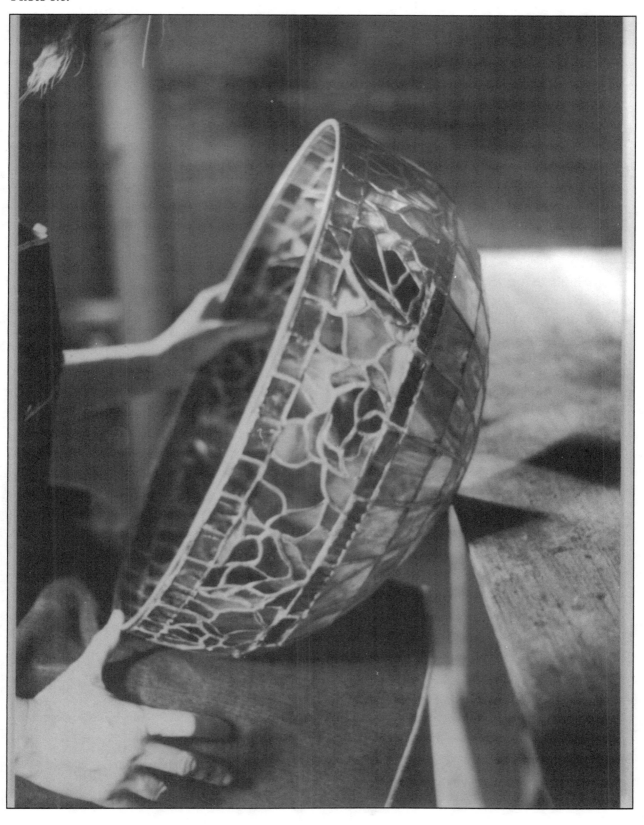

THE LAMPMAKING HANDBOOK

melt the solder or smooth the joint using a fine-tooth file. The latter technique is advisable to avoid overheating the area and possibly separating one or both of the ends. With the leading completed, the shade can now be prepared for the patina

Patina

The traditional definition of patina differs somewhat from what we consider it today. Originally, patina was specifically the fine green rust with which ancient bronzes and copper coins and metals became covered by lying in particular soils; it was both preservative and ornamental. In the contemporary decorative metal arts, any artificial coloring of the metal surface, or chemical acceleration of the naturally occurring oxidation process is known as patina, or patination. Fine patina work has traditionally belonged to the alchemist, someone who could produce gold from base materials, so to speak, given the high value of those metal works displaying a fine, subtly colored patina. The wonderful coloristic nuances of fine patina on metals have always been shrouded in mystery, secrecy and what was thought to be magic. Pragmatically, success with patinas has always been the result of extensive research, development, trial, error, expense and skill. Without instruction manuals on the subject though, these prized formulas and techniques were handed down from one craftsperson to another as a kind of valuable inheritance, to be guarded from the unworthy.

It is no surprise to find that artists and firms known for their fine patinas, assign "Top Secret" status to their chemical recipes. Some firms and individuals specialize exclusively in applying patina to metals. If they produce consistently high quality results, they are very sought after and their services are very valuable.

A natural looking patina is achieved by a gradual oxidation of the metal surface and the

Photo 8.7:

manipulation of chemical additives known to produce certain color effects on metal. Oxidation is the chemical change that gives rise to oxides; it is brought about by the action of oxygen, acids and water. Artists and craftspeople are interested in the artificial reproduction of this action through the use of chemicals, heat, water and/or electrochemical processes.

Coloring metals is not an exact science. As proficient as one can be in producing a fine patina on metal, certain factors and variables will always enter in, and these factors influence the various coloring effects. Metal alloys (like solder) react differently to coloring agents than do metals of high integrity, such as brass, copper and bronze. The more you know about the composition of the metal, the better prepared you will be to govern its reactions to a given patina solution.

The temperature of the metal and the chemical applied will influence the final result. The amount of time the chemical agent is allowed to work and the purity of that agent also have to be considered. The condition of the underlying metal and whether it has been properly cleaned will produce varied, if not unpredictable, colorings. Another factor that can affect the patina is the climate of the work area. Because patinas form from an oxidizing process, humidity becomes a factor in the process.

Considering the variables, how does one go about achieving a quality patina on a stained glass lamp? Like any other technical aspect of a craft, the more knowledge, understanding and experience you gather, the better equipped you will be to produce consistent and predictable results. Simply stated, practice makes perfect. Metal coloring is an arena where even the most experienced professionals are constantly improving and refining their craft. It is a constant pursuit to find faster and more effective ways of controlling the elusive aspects of patina.

Because the goal of this book is to make the entire lampmaking process more accessible, there is no extended discussion of commercial

electroplating. Instead, the chemical treatment of the metals is explained in effort to keep the process in the studio. That is not to say that a lampmaker should not consider such services as commercial electroplating. Indeed, a qualified electroplator can be relied upon for consistent and reliable results, if at a (sometimes healthy) price.

You can avoid the added expense of commercial electroplating. Through experimentation and practice with metal coloring solutions available from conventional sources, excellent results can be achieved. Such in-house procedures also eliminate the time involved in sending work out for electroplating. Some firms require a two-week turnaround for lamps.

The techniques described here are the results of extensive trial-and-error. The minimal amount of information published to date on the subject leaves trial and error as the only recourse for the artist in search of an efficient studio patina. Be prepared for variations even if you follow the directions and guidelines perfectly. Where variations can occur, solutions or alternatives will be suggested.

Starting The Process

It is best to have a result in mind when applying a patina, even if it is a very vague idea. You may admire the traditional brownish-green of Tiffany lamps or the reddish-brown of Remington sculptures. A black patina may be the final enhancement of a modernist piece or you may simply desire the golden shine of polished copper, both of which can be achieved with a single chemical application. With an ideal in mind, you will be prepared to manipulate or stop the process when the desired color is achieved. You will not be at the mercy of the metal's reaction to the treatment and the cumulative nature (increasing intensity) of some patina solutions. Lamps are usually married to a base whose patina can be used as a model for the metalwork on the lamp. Even a photograph can serve as a model, provided it is clear and the color of the metal surface can be discerned. The point is to establish a goal and proceed from there.

The following procedures describe the patination process. Three different types of patina finishes will be discussed: a simple, bright copper-gold patina; an antique pewter or black patina; and a more involved brownish-green Tiffany patina.

Cleaning The Metal

One of the most important facts to remember is that a coloring agent will reflect the quality and condition of the underlying metal surface. This is always true. If the underlying surface is dirty, greasy or otherwise impure, it will compromise the success of the patina. If the underlying color is uneven or improperly applied, subsequent applications of coloring agents will reflect these imperfections. Never lose sight of this.

Patina should be applied as soon as possible after final soldering. The reason for this is simple; lead/tin solders begin to oxidize as soon as they cool. The oxidation may not be immediately visible, but it's happening. The longer the lead lines are left untreated, the more intense this unwanted oxidation becomes, and it is cumulative. Any patina, with the exception of pewter black, will suffer if exposed to this oxidation. A work left overnight usually will not oxidize to the point where remedial steps need to be taken. Nevertheless, be aware of it.

Lead/tin solders that oxidize will lose their silvery sheen and become dull. Further oxidation will produce a white powdery substance along the edges of the solder lines, which will eventually invade the entire surface of the bead. Some of this oxidation can be removed with abrasives such as steel wool, or with an application of a pumice-and-water solution which is then rinsed off. Seriously oxidized surfaces may require serious remedial action or electroplating, a process best left to professionals.

With this in mind, we can begin the process by cleaning the metal; the lead/tin solder and any brass or copper hardware or reinforcing metals that were added to the structure.

The goal of cleaning is to remove any flux, dirt or grease from the metal surface. If no oxidation has occurred, a simple rinse with warm water and a hand-held bristle brush will suffice. A mild detergent can also be applied, but must be completely rinsed away, as any compound remaining on the surface of the metal will react with the coloring agent and will produce unpredictable results.

Wipe the entire surface dry with paper towels after rinsing, being careful not to handle the metal surfaces too much. Avoid placing the cleaned work on any unclean surface, such as a worktable that has been soiled with flux.

Copper-Gold Patina

This very popular patina is relatively easy to produce. Many prepared copper sulfate solutions are available and will provide excellent results if properly applied. Raw crystals and powders of copper sulfate can be purchased by those who prefer to mix their own solutions. Copper sulfate can usually be mixed with clear tap water. Altering the sulfate-to-water ratio will produce solutions of greater or lesser strength. Those who wish to experiment with such solutions should be prepared to go through a good deal of trial and error. All such experiments should be done on sample panels. For the purposes at hand, all chemicals were pre-mixed by the manufacturers.

Having cleaned the lamp, place it in a plastic tub larger than the piece itself. This receptacle should not be made out of any material, such as metal, that will react to the patina solution. Plastic is suitable.

When working with patina solutions, you should have a pair of elbow-length neoprene or nitrile gloves (see chapter 10). Get into the practice of donning these gloves no matter which patina or cleaning solution you are working with. You will never regret being safe.

Place a small amount of copper-sulfate solution into a separate plastic receptacle. Apply the liquid to the surface of the lamp with a paper towel, or brush the patina directly onto the lead lines and metal surfaces with a grouting brush. If the solder lines have been properly cleaned, the solution will have an immediate and obvious effect. If any sections of the work do not accept the color, there may be some residual dirt or grease on the surface. Carefully clean these areas with a fine grade steel wool, buff clean to remove any steel-wool filings and re-apply the solution. Rinse the lamp with water once you've achieved an acceptable color. Dispose of any patina solution remaining in the plastic basin in which the lamp was treated. A note about patina disposal: Most patinas and related solutions (i.e., flux or caustic metal cleaners) are considered toxic waste by local, state and federal environmental protection agencies. Be sure to follow all applicable guidelines when disposing of such materials and never just flush these chemicals down the drain, especially if your home is connected to a septic system.

The patina's finish can be highlighted with a wax cleaner, such as *Simichrome* polish. Apply the polish with a cloth and buff to a high luster.

Pewter Or Black Patina

Pewter or black patinas are just as easy to apply as copper sulfate. Pewter finishes are distinguished by a charcoal-grey tone as opposed to the deeper black of antique black patina. These coloring solutions are extremely fast-acting; one application will normally be enough. Remember to wear safety equipment (gloves, apron and respirator) whenever you are handling coloring agents.

In a plastic basin larger than the lamp being treated, blot the patina onto the shade's surface with a rag or paper towel. Be sure to cover all the metal areas, including aperture, edge hard-

ware and any reinforcing metals. An abrasive treatment, such as that with a grout brush, is unnecessary with these solutions; the metal will color immediately upon receiving the solution without any abrasive action. Once applied, rinse the work. The rinse will stop the action of the solution. You can now use a glass cleaner to clean the metal and glass.

Simichrome and other polishes must be used carefully on pewter and antique black patinas, as they have been known to actually remove these finishes. If you want to use a wax polish, test it first on a sample.

Darkeners are notorious for their tendency to stain anything and everything with which they come in contact. Consequently, do not rinse the lamp in a kitchen sink; darkeners have been known to permanently stain basins. Again, you should not be rinsing your work in a regular sink as you must dispose of the solutions in an environmentally sound way. Check with the chemical manufacturer.

Tiffany Brown-Green

The most desirable patina coloring, the Tiffany brown-green, is the most difficult to achieve. Where other patinas stain on contact, this patina and its variants require a series of surface treatments. Counting preparation, applications, other procedures and drying time, a session with this patina can easily extend from three to six hours. The time taken depends on the size of the work being treated, the skill of the craftsperson, the tint desired and the environmental conditions in the studio. Be prepared for a lengthy process.

Read through the following procedures carefully, more than once if necessary. Familiarize yourself with the different stages of coloring and try to visualize each application as you proceed. When you understand how the treatment progresses from one step to the next, practice. It is a good idea to assemble a sample panel, on which you can experiment.

Follow the procedures carefully and remember that variations will occur with each individual situation and environment. Trial and error is the key principle here. Where variations and potential problems may be encountered, remedies or alternatives will be suggested.

The procedures that follow involve chemicals that are considerably more toxic and potentially harmful than those mentioned earlier. Take precautions to secure a safe work environment and avoid personal injury. Read about patinas in the chapter 10 before you begin.

Step 1: Copper Plating

Copper plating solutions operate as effective substitutes to commercial electroplating. Professional plating always involves expense that can add a great deal to the cost of the finished work. A chemical alternative applied in the studio also eliminates the time a piece spends at the plator's.

The solution used in the following process is called "Copper Plating Solution" by the manufacturer. (Most manufacturers adhere to simple descriptions of metal coloring solutions). It is a blue-green, water-based solution that contains sulfuric acid. The presence of sulfuric acid necessitates proper safety precautions in handling and storage. Do not proceed if you don't have the correct safety gear or if your studio is not properly equipped. These precautions cannot be taken lightly and by no means should they be neglected. Before using this solution, observe the following safety precautions:

- Neoprene or nitrile gloves must be worn when handling this solution. These type of gloves are designed for heavy-duty industrial applications. They provide resistance to solvents, acids and alcohols and are durable enough to protect against all manner of cuts, abrasions and punctures. They are essential here.

- Wear a respirator equipped with replaceable filters. Keep area ventilation active. An exchange of air is the best kind of ventilation. This involves exhausting studio air and introducing fresh air.

- Wear clear safety glasses as protection from any splashes of patina solution.

- Follow the manufacturer's safety and emergency guidelines as per their MSDS (Material Safety Data Sheet).

- Contain and dispose of all chemicals as instructed by the manufacturer and regulated by state and local governments. You will have to contact the EPA or local environmental agencies, as well as the fire department, to determine safe disposal procedures in accordance with regulations.

- Never mix chemicals from different manufacturers. The results can be extremely violent and dangerous.

- Use the smallest practical amounts of any chemical. It is easier to add solution than to deal with and dispose of large amounts.

- Store chemicals per the manufacturer's instructions and according to the guidelines of state and local departments of environmental protection and local fire codes.

- Do not buy chemicals from manufacturers who do not supply safety information, MSDSs. The law requires they supply MSDSs for all their products.

- Do not work in family areas. Keep all chemical activities properly segregated from living spaces such as kitchens, dining areas, playrooms, etc. Above all, keep all chemicals away from children, pregnant women and pets.

Your lamp has now been properly cleaned, you have taken all the proper safety precautions, and are now ready to treat the work with the first application of coloring solution. You will need a small putty or grouting brush, or any small, soft-bristled brush, a roll of paper towels, a plastic basin, fine-gauge steel wool and somewhere to rinse the shade. Label the bristle brush with the type of patina. Do not use the same brush for applying different chemicals.

Pour a small amount of Copper Plating Solution into a plastic basin. Brush the solution onto the surface of the shade by first soaking the bristles in the solution. This will keep the amount of solution down to a minimum, while reducing the likelihood of it splashing around the work area.

There will be two separate applications of this solution. Brush the patina onto the shade's surface with a quick back-and-forth motion, covering all glass and metal. As you apply this first coat, you will see an immediate reaction. The solder lines and metal surfaces will turn a splotchy yellow-orange and the consistency of the finish will be highly irregular; this is perfectly natural. It is the nature of this process and the treatment of some metals that the second application always produces a better effect than the first one.

Once the first coat of solution has been applied to all surfaces, rinse the lamp in warm water. This will remove any excess solution from the work and allow preparation for the second application. Allow the work to air dry completely before the next step.

When the shade is dry, take a pad of fine steel wool and remove the first coat of solution completely with a back-and-forth brushing motion. Although this step might seem strange, it is necessary. The first application has "bitten into"

the metal surfaces, preparing them to better accept the second coat of solution. All evidence of the first application should be removed. The lead lines should look as they did before the first application. Once this is done, rinse the work again to remove any residual steel wool filings. If they remain on the surface, they will interfere with the next application. Blot the work dry.

The second coat is applied in exactly the same way as the first. This coat will produce a vivid and consistent orange-copper color if the shade has been properly cleaned and dried. The finish will be unlike the gold-copper of conventional copper sulfate patina. The color will appear immediately.

Rinse the work as soon as a satisfactory coating has been achieved. Allowing the solution to sit on the metal surfaces for an extended period of time will affect the quality and nature of the color. Rinsing will stop the action of the solution and "lock on" the resulting color.

The next step is optional, but recommended. To produce a fine luster on the colored metal, you need to remember that all coloring agents reflect the condition of the underlying metal. This second coat of copper plating solution can be polished before any further coloring is done. A lamb's wool buffing pad attached to an electric hand drill is best for buffing. It is a fast and simple process. Just pass the wool pad over the surface of the work. Begin on either the inside or the outside of the shade, but remember to buff all surfaces, ring and aperture included. Once this is done, you can begin darkening the copper plated undercoat.

Step 2: Darkening

Darken the copper plated lead lines with Brown Darkener (as it is called by the manufacturer). This solution gradually deepens the copper tone and will continue to do so until the action is arrested by rinsing. During this process, it is essential to have a definite idea of how deep and rich the resulting tone should be.

A sample, either physical or photographic, of the desired brown patina should be kept on hand to govern and guide the coloring process.

Clean all receptacles of any residual chemical solution. Carefully wipe up any spills. Do not remove your safety equipment or stop any auxiliary ventilation. Pour a small amount of brown darkener into a clean plastic basin. Use a clean bristle brush and, with the same procedure used to apply the copper plating solution, apply the darkener. Be sure to cover all metal areas. This will impart an even and consistent color to the metal surfaces.

Brown darkener does not produce immediate results, in fact, as it is being applied, nothing happens at all. Once you've coated all areas, set the work aside but not out of eyesight. You must monitor the progress of the darkener as it gradually works upon the copper plated metal.

The color produced by this darkener over a properly applied copper plated base ranges from a slightly deepened copper tone to a rich brown. The brown is a result of the longest exposure to the solution. Once you acquire a pleasing tone (the longest exposure should be no more than 10 to 20 minutes) the action of the brown darkener can be stopped by simply rinsing the work in clear tap water. Wipe the lamp dry before buffing the metal surfaces to a soft luster. The work is now ready for application of the green patina.

Step 3: Green Patina

Achieving a green patina is a cumulative process and one that depends on a strong copper base. It is also the most unpredictable metal coloring procedure and the one most affected by environmental conditions, such as room temperature and humidity. Trial and error is the only way to master the greening process.

Having achieved a suitable brownish tone, prepare the lamp to receive the green patina. Clean all receptacles and blot dry any spills that may have occurred. Do not remove any safety equipment or neglect any safety precautions.

Use a bristle brush designated for use only with green patina.

Pour a small amount of the solution into a clean plastic basin. Soak the bristles and then begin brushing the metal with a brisk, back-and-forth motion, being sure to cover all areas. The patina will produce no immediate reaction.

Continue brushing until the solution produces a dull, grayish film on the metal. This film will appear first on the brass, or copper hardware and then on the treated solder lines. The appearance of this film is desirable, as it is visual evidence that the green patina is indeed reacting with the underlying metal. It will not be evident in the final color.

Having properly treated the work, set it aside (again within sight, as the action of the patina needs to be monitored to be kept under control). After a short time, usually 10 to 15 minutes, small amounts of green color should appear in random areas of the shade. As the solution dries further, more green will appear. Do not rinse the work. The solution needs to dry completely before any other chemical or sealant is applied (this is peculiar to the green patina).

If a satisfactory green was achieved with the first application, apply no additional solution. If a deeper or more intense green is desired, repeat the process. In adding to an existing green patina, re-application will seem to remove the original green color. This is normal. The second application produces a stronger and more widespread green, regardless of how it affects the first.

Some tints of green will require up to three applications of patina. You will have to judge for yourself when to stop the action of the solution. Allow each successive application of green patina to dry thoroughly between coats. As with the browning stage, it is advisable to have a goal in mind; a tint or depth of green that, when achieved, can be stopped.

Rinse the work to stop the action of the patina. Do not rub the surface; let the work air dry. Any abrasive action on the metal work may remove some of the green as long as the work is still wet and the patina is still vulnerable.

If any filmy residue appears on the shade, especially on the glass while it is drying, blot it clean with a paper towel (being careful not to disturb the green color on the metal). White blotches may appear on the solder lines, these are salts that develop during the coloring process. These salts may or may not appear in the course of a patina session. If they do appear, they will usually do so as the patina is drying. These blotches are highly undesirable and need to be removed from the work as they become evident. If left alone, they will dry onto the surface, after which they will be very difficult to remove. To remove them, simply blot with a damp paper towel, or gently rub with a Q-tip.

When the desired degree of green has been produced and the work has dried completely, rinse with clear tap water and allow to air dry. Do not rub the surface when rinsing. The green patina is most durable only after it has completely dried.

Waxing

Any patina can be protected and enhanced by a final coat of clear lacquer sealant and wax buffed to a soft shine. Both are available in hardware stores and home centers. Each is quite easily applied.

A sprayed-on coat of clear lacquer will create a barrier between the colored metal surface and any oxidizing agents in the atmosphere, thus securing a fine patina and protecting the investment of time and effort necessary to produce it. Spray in a well ventilated area and according to the manufacturer's instructions. Cover all areas of the work, first inside, then out. A coat of lacquer is not apparent on the work's surface. It doesn't create any unsightly buildup if it is applied evenly, allowing no drips, runs or puddles. Once the lacquer has dried, preferably overnight, a finishing wax can be applied.

To apply paste wax, add a small amount of

the wax to a soft cloth. Gently rub the wax onto the surface of the lamp, covering all metal and glass areas. Wax both the inside and outside of the shade. Let the wax stand for about 10 to 15 minutes. Buff to a shine with a soft cloth or a lamb's wool buffing wheel. The shine will come up immediately.

Choosing A Base

A stained glass shade is enhanced by an appropriate base. Are there guidelines to follow in choosing the right base for the work? Are proportions set in hard and fast rules? Yes and no.

Obviously, a small 16" diameter lamp will look ridiculous on a large floor base. Conversely, a 28" shade demands the support of a tall floor base. Although extreme examples, the same considerations apply to both. The diameter of the shade in relation to the height of the base is the basis for a proper marriage of the two. This is plain aesthetic sense.

When reproducing an existing shade and base, the decisions have already been made (provided the base is currently available). If the base is not available, the proportions of the original can easily be matched with a base similar in size and shape.

Hundreds of lamp bases are available in a variety of styles and sizes; Victorian, Art Nouveau, Art Deco, even some that defy description. The important considerations in choosing a base are:

1. Proportion to the shade in height and platform diameter.

2. Construction and metal type of the base.

3. How it supports the shade.

4. The configuration of the light sources.

There are some general rules to determine the correct proportion of height to diameter. First, the diameter of the base should be no more than two-thirds of the shade's diameter and no less than one third. Bases with a larger diameter will look bottom-heavy; those with a smaller diameter will look top-heavy and will not provide suitable support. Within these guidelines, you can easily and immediately eliminate a number of possibilities.

There are exceptions to these guidelines. The most obvious being the Tiffany Wisteria lamp on its Tree Trunk Base. Here, a lamp 18" in diameter sits upon a base whose platform diameter approaches 16". What saves the marriage is the tapered diameter of the base. From a diameter of more than 1" where the platform rises into the stem, the base gradually tapers in the same way tree branches gradually blend into the surrounding landscape.

In some instances, if a lamp is very deep it can sustain placement on a base that might otherwise be too big, or generally more suitable to a shade of larger diameter. The added depth works to increase the upper mass of the marriage, thus adjusting to the eye what, under other proportions would look like a mismatch. A case in point would be a 16" diameter shade with a depth of 9" or more, mounted onto a base that would normally support a 20" lamp.

Experience will always be the best teacher in developing an instinctive feel for lamp-to-base proportions. As you familiarize yourself with examples that elicit a favorable response from you and viewers, you will formulate a mental library and reference guide to proper and improper choices. Rather than having to physically mount every shade upon a base to determine compatibility, you will envision the proper proportions and make your choices based on your developing principles. More often than not, marriages of lamp and base that are pleasing to you, will be pleasing to others. The reverse is also true.

Other factors can also affect the visual impact of a shade and base combination. The mass of the base's stem can add to or deter from the total

look. The shape of the shade, whether it is conical, dome-shaped, or geometric will dictate what is to be placed beneath it. And finally, the style or period of the lamp's artwork needs to be appropriate to the base.

Indeed, there are many considerations in matching shade to base. These variables and personal preference make base selection less than an exact science. The few guidelines that do exist can be applied, but the best guideline is a well developed sense of beauty and proportion. This sense can be nurtured and developed by simply studying existing lamp-to-base combinations, especially those that appear most pleasing to the eye. Lamp-base combinations that appear awkward, top- or bottom-heavy, too high or too low, will call out for correction like wrong notes in a musical passage. Highly decorative lamps supported by bases that are overladen with decoration will clash in the same way mismatched decorative elements of an interior design might. Well crafted lamps certainly look entirely out of place atop cheap, gaudy bases.

By taking mental notes of the combinations that are not appealing, we can better choose those that are. This will create a vocabulary of workable shapes and proportions that we can then use and translate into successful shade-to-base combinations.

Original Tiffany shades were seldom mismatched to their bases. The Tiffany artists and craftspeople, in both the glassworking and metal working departments were well trained and very keen to the proper marriage of base and shade. They even developed certain bases specifically for one shade design or diameter. Even though many of the bases could be mixed and matched to the shades, the bases were grouped according to the size of shade they would properly support.

Many of Tiffany's contemporaries took their lead from the products of his studios, copying his lamps in concept and proportion. Studying the works of lampmaking studios such as

Handel and Duffner and Kimberly, adds to your visual experience and vocabulary of workable lamp-base combinations.

By seeking out books, catalogs and museum collections where these lamps can be viewed and studied, you will develop a library of shapes and forms that work well together. With such ammunition, you can match a shade and base with increasing confidence. Check the bibliography for some excellent reference books.

A variety of lamp base types and styles are available to lampmakers. Depending on certain qualities of style and workmanship, these bases can range from $50 to over $1,000. As lamp makers and lampmaking expand, more styles and types in all price categories will appear.

White Metal Bases

These usually represent the low end, or most affordable of lamp bases. White metal is a very inexpensive metal to cast and re-work, making the mass manufacture of these bases possible both domestically and abroad. Available styles range from simple standards devoid of decoration, to the most elaborate and sometimes overworked Victorian styles. Sizes range from under 12" to floorlamp height. Quality of finish and patina vary from burnished brass, to brass, to black, to faux bronze. Bases can also be found that incorporate other materials, such as marble and onyx into their structure.

Brass Bases

Brass bases represent a higher quality metal, workmanship and finish than white metal; differences reflected in the higher price. The most striking brass bases are finished with highly polished and lacquered surfaces, giving the bases a shine that may or may not be appealing. These bases look best supporting a shade that complements the bright brass finish. Some copper patinas are compatible with a high-polish brass base. Most darkened finishes are not.

Styles vary from traditional to contemporary.

Imported Reproduction Bases

These bases provide good value in style, design and compatibility with traditional stained glass shades, as most are copied from Tiffany or Tiffany-style originals. These are most commonly copper-plated brass castings finished in variations of a bronze-green patina. The quality of the castings and patina, evident by the crispness of surface detail and the lack of pitholes and flash (excess) metal in the casting, vary from almost acceptable to very good. Prices start around $100 and represent good value in terms of quality and visual appeal.

Bronze Bases

A small number of bronze bases made to strict Tiffany quality standards are produced in this country. They are carefully cast and crafted to perfectly match the original in every detail. Decorative applications are applied by hand, all components are separately cast and the patina is applied through a very elaborate and time-consuming process. These masterworks in metal rival the shades in terms of craftsmanship and labor intensity, qualities reflected in their price. It is interesting to note that in the showroom catalogs of the Tiffany Studios, the prices of the bases often equalled those of the shades. In some instances, they exceeded the price of the works in glass. This holds true today for high quality bronze reproductions.

Mounting

The best support for a shade mounted on a base is the traditional Tiffany method of spider, ring and cap. With this system, the lamp's aperture ring rests on the spider's metal flange and the spider is mounted onto the top of the base by means of a threaded nipple. This rests the shade securely on the base, discouraging the tilting and tipping that occurs with a fixed cap with one single point of support. This support from underneath the shade is ideal. Anytime you can reproduce this system you guarantee better stability for your work.

Hanging Lamps

Almost any lamp, with the exception of those of a very small diameter, can be hung rather than placed on a base. The most important consideration is the weight of the shade and the area that must bear that weight—the aperture. Any hanging lamp is suspended from its aperture opening. If this area is not properly reinforced with a correctly sized metal fixture it will not support the weight of the shade.

A hanging shade is best supported from underneath. A spider or wheel supporting the shade on an aperture ring mounted on its lip or flange will distribute the shade's weight throughout the perimeter of the aperture. When a metal cap is just soldered to the aperture opening the shade is supported by a single stress point. Because a more substantial aperture ring has little chance of pulling away from the structure, due to its considerable mass and durable solder joint, it is better prepared to bear the weight of the shade. Caps milled from thin sheets of brass cannot support the downward weight of the shade. They will gradually pull away from their soldered joints, causing considerable damage and presenting a very hazardous situation, especially if the buildup of heat from the interior light cluster is excessive.

A chain will be needed to hang the lamp. The chain should be proportionate to the size of the shade. Most conventional chain suffices unless the size of the shade approaches the unusual.

Any lamp larger than 22" should be hung with extreme caution. The chain should be sufficiently secured to a ceiling beam and not simply hanging from a butterfly bolt installed in sheet rock. Any chain used in supporting larger shades must be able to support the added weight without having its links extend and separate over time.

Light Sources

Very little light is necessary to activate stained glass in a lamp. In fact, subtle lighting enhances the dramatic quality of the finer glasses. Fight the urge to overload a lamp with the maximum amount of bulb wattage. Three or more bulb sockets does not mean you can install three 100-watt bulbs into the fixture. High wattage bulbs build up enough heat to gradually soften and compromise the strength of the solder lines and joints. A good rule of thumb in detecting excessive heat buildup within a shade is to touch the area of the shade where the bulbs come closest to the glass. If the glass is too hot to touch, it is too hot for the lead and solder joints as well. Reduce the wattage of the bulbs.

Lamps of a larger diameter require more light, but the same rules apply and the same dangers exist where unnecessary amounts of heat build up. Large lamps also have increased weight, which can compound any structural problems caused by heat buildup. Any lighting fixture, lamp base, or electrical addition must be UL listed. Any products not displaying the appropriate seal should be rejected.

Should any aspect of wiring or hanging an electrical lamp or fixture fall beyond your experience, abilities or desires, seek professional help from a licensed electrician. ■

9

Designing Your Own Lamp

The future of lampmaking lies in new and original works, creations that go beyond the traditional. No creative form can prosper and develop by constantly reproducing existing designs. Looking to the past for instruction and guidance in discovering or rediscovering lampmaking is fine and necessary to a certain extent, but new designs and ideas are needed to keep lampmaking "alive" as a valid medium of individual artistic expression.

Designing for lampmaking is very much like mastering a new craft. The blank mold must first be prepared as a drawing surface. The image, once drawn with proper composition and size, must be transferred onto the mold's surface and a master layout and working templates must be produced from that design.

Design Choices

Almost any image can be adapted to a lamp design. If an idea can be graphically portrayed, it can usually be translated into a lamp design. Mastering the design procedure will open up the possibilities of your own personal aesthetic.

Choose a relatively simple idea for your first project. The purpose at hand is learning lamp design; do not complicate your introduction to design techniques with a design that may frustrate your efforts. Once you have mastered the techniques, involve your imagination to any extent you desire.

A simple floral design supported on a geometric background is a good place to start learning lamp design and layout. This configuration will introduce you to the two major elements of lamp design, straight and curved lines. This will also acquaint you with the traditional type of lamp that you may already have experience with. You will be able to relate your newly developed design techniques to the finished pieces you have executed using prepared designs. Keeping it simple will allow you to progress at a good pace.

In choosing your design look for the following qualities in your prospective choices:

Flowers: Multi-petaled flowers will better lend themselves to creating patterns or templates. They will conform better to the curvature of the mold, and offer greater possibilities of glass selection and color.

Size Of Design Elements: Choose subjects that will not suffer from the changes that may be necessary to adapt them for use on a lamp. For example, long, narrow elements will, in most cases, have to be broken into many pieces to accommodate the curvature of the mold. This may compromise the quality of the design. On the other hand, subjects that incorporate many tiny elements may prove too busy and will have to be simplified.

A Simple Design: Avoid the temptation to overload the surface of the mold with a tight, complex image at this time. Once you are familiar with lamp design, increase the complexity of your design. You may find, as you progress, that simplicity is far more pleasing for some particular shapes and lamp sizes.

Color Possibilities: Always choose subject matter offering the greatest color possibilities, especially where building multiples of the same lamp is intended. A design element or theme with a limited color range will prove boring when repeated.

Quality Of Art Work: Choose designs that will not tax your artistic abilities. Do not frustrate your efforts with artwork that you cannot comfortably execute. Remember, this is your first design for a stained glass lamp. You are concerned with learning how to apply a design and master the necessary techniques. Familiarize yourself with the design process. Read through the following procedures before designing your own lamp. You will need the following tools to transfer your design onto the mold:

- A roll of ½" masking tape
- Pencils
- Protractor
- Compass
- Calipers
- A Flexible curve
- Several fine-point permanent markers

- 2 single-edge razor blades
- A sheet of clear or frosted acetate
- A pair of scissors

Design Techniques

With the mold placed directly in front of you on the worktable, cover the surface with a layer of masking tape as follows: Begin at any point at the top of the mold, extend a single length of masking tape from the top to the bottom of the mold. Proceeding around the form from left to right, continue placing vertical strips of tape, overlapping each previous strip about ¼" as you progress. Overlapping the strips of tape will allow you to later remove the resulting template in one piece (see photo 9.1).

Cover more of the surface than you intend to use. For example, if you plan for your design to cover one third of the surface, resulting in a three-way repeat of the design, cover more than one third of the form with masking tape (two inches of additional space on either side will suffice). This excess will allow you the extra drawing surface needed to properly create the return of the design.

If you have not yet chosen the diameter of the aperture opening, and the mold or form you are using does not have one established, do it now. Using a compass with its pointer set at the center of the top of the mold, draw a circle to the desired diameter. Keep the measurement simple (i.e., 3", 4", etc.), fractional measurements will only create problems when fitting hardware to the finished lamp. Make all markings in pencil to facilitate any corrections that may be necessary.

Establish the upper parameters of the return using a protractor. You know that the circle you've just drawn at the top of the mold represents 360 degrees. If you decide to create a design that repeats three times, each return represents 120 degrees (360 degrees divided by three. Four-way returns represent 90 degrees each, and so on.

For the following, refer to Illus. 9.1. Fix the centerpoint of your protractor to the centerpoint of the aperture Point A. Align one zero radius to a point on the newly drawn circle, and make a mark where the radius intersects the perimeter, Point B. Keeping the protractor in position, find the desired degree marking, in this case 120 degrees, and make a similar mark at that radius along the aperture, Point C. The upper boundaries of one third of the mold's surface have now been established.

Vertical lines need to be drawn from points A and B. The lines must extend down the entire surface of the mold and be perfectly perpendicular to the aperture's perimeter. You will need a compass and a flexible curve to accomplish this.

Extend the compass approximately ¾" (an exact measurement is not necessary). Fix the point of the compass onto point B. Make an intersecting arc along the aperture's perimeter on either side of the fixed point, creating points D and E (see Photo. 9.2). Remove the compass and increase its extension to approximately

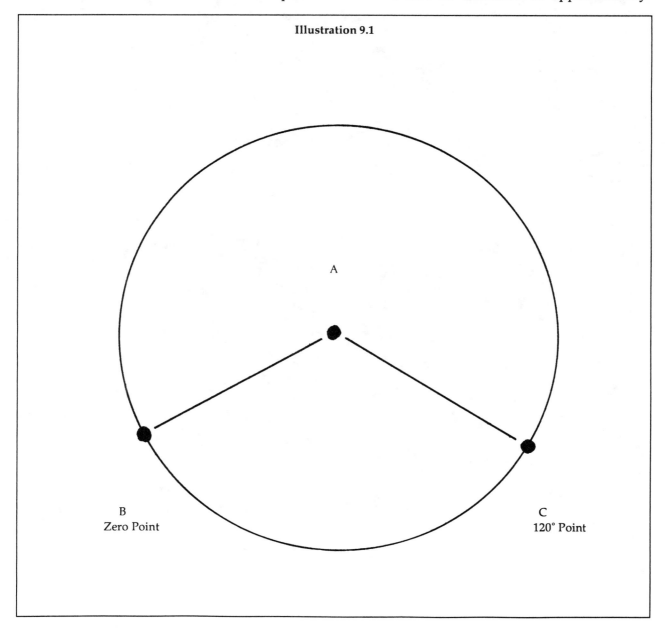

Illustration 9.1

A

B
Zero Point

C
120° Point

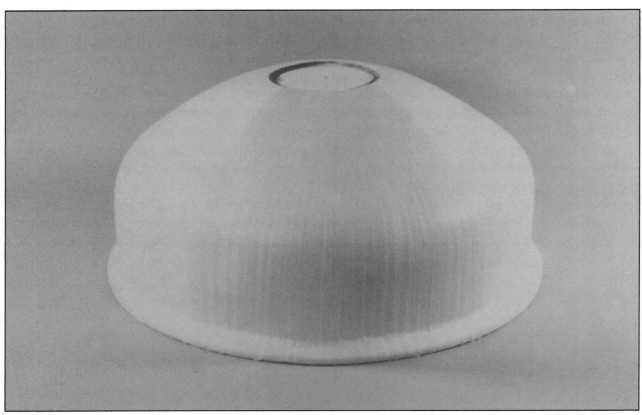

Photo 9.1

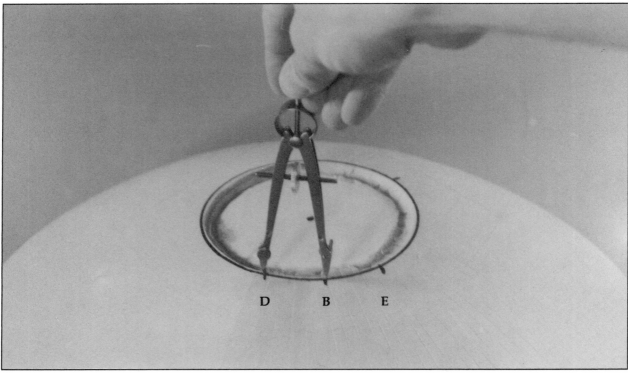

Photo 9.2.

1½" to 2". Again, an exact measurement is not necessary. Fix the compass point to Point D and draw an arc directly under Point A. Allow the line to sweep about 3" long (see Photo 9.3). Remove the compass from this position and repeat the procedure from Point E. The two new arcs should intersect, creating Point F (see Photo. 9.4).

Take a flexible curve and position it against the mold, aligning the edge with Points B and F. Draw a line connecting these two points, extending through Point F to the bottom of the mold, line G (see Photo. 9.5). This perpendicular line will represent one boundary of our design section. Repeat this procedure from Point E. The resulting line from Point E represents the opposite boundary and establishes a one-third section (see Photo. 9.6). We can now to transfer the design onto the surface.

If you desire a geometric row at the top of your design, now is the time to draw it onto the mold. First measure and mark the desired width of the geometric row down from the aperture (⅜", ½", etc.). Place the compass' pointer end at the center of the top of the mold. Extend the drawing end until it meets the mark establishing the width of the row. Draw a circle (see Photo 9.7).

To create a line of brick-like pieces for this geometric row, use a caliper to mark equal sections from one vertical edge to the other. Use your flexible curve to create the pieces by lining it up from the center point of the mold to the marks made by the caliper (see Photo 9.8).

Drawing On The Mold

Whether you are drawing your image freehand or tracing it from another design source, observe the following guidelines:

1. Place and draw your primary design elements (flowers, for instance) first. Follow with secondary images, such as leaves, stems and buds. Design borders last. Don't break up background areas until all your major design elements have been placed.

2. Draw from left to right. Allow your image to bleed past the vertical boundary for the entire distance down the left side of the mold. Do not erase the left vertical boundary; it must appear through the design. This line will be used to accurately position the design onto the right side of the mold when creating another "return" (see photo 9.9).

3. On the right side of the mold, leave at least 1" of clear space to the left of the vertical boundary. This allows you to create the repeating section. This procedure will be explained shortly.

4. Make all drawings in pencil, so corrections can be easily made.

5. Straight bottom borders are drawn, if necessary, by first measuring a small distance up from the bottom of the mold. This is done at a number of points on the drawing surface. With the flexible curve held in a horizontal position, connect these points. The resulting horizontal line represents the new bottom border of the design. You may also allow the bottom edge of the mold to establish the design's boundary.

6. Keep the curvature of the mold in mind as you draw your image onto the surface. Large pieces will be unstable as they are placed onto the flat surface, creating unsightly sharp peaks of glass once assembled. Glass should assume the shape of the form. Once cut, the pieces should sit almost flat on the curved surface. Test a small piece of glass against the mold to determine what size sits most comfortably without wobbling.

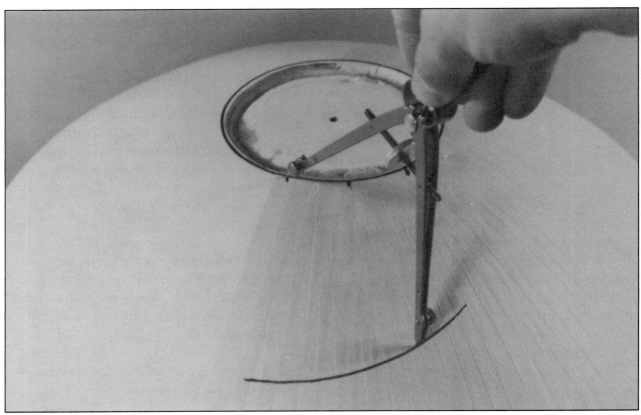

Photo 9.3

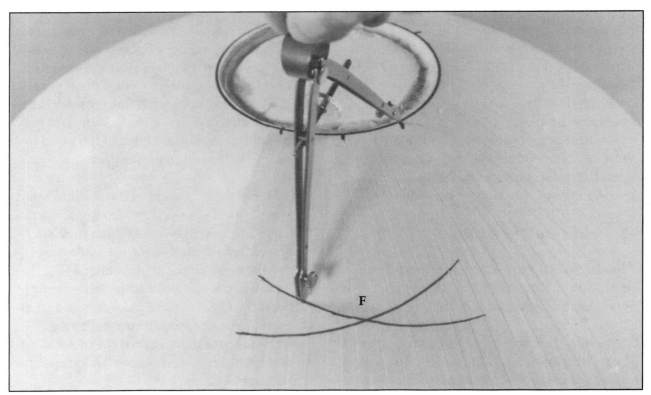

Photo 9.4

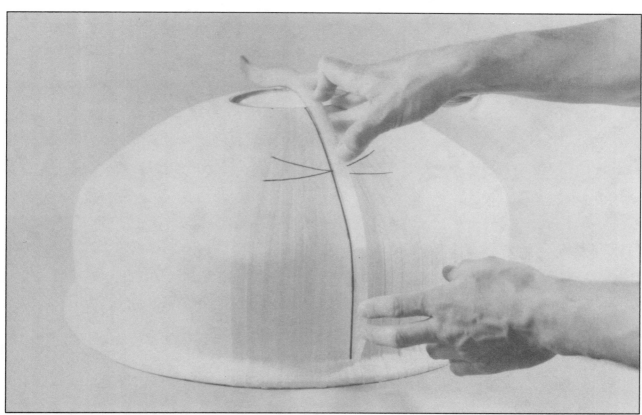

Photo 9.5

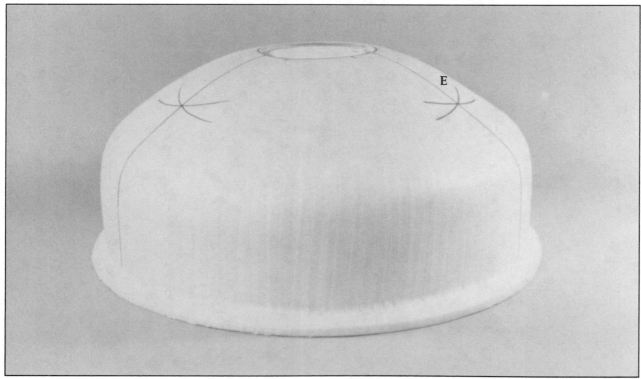

Photo 9.6

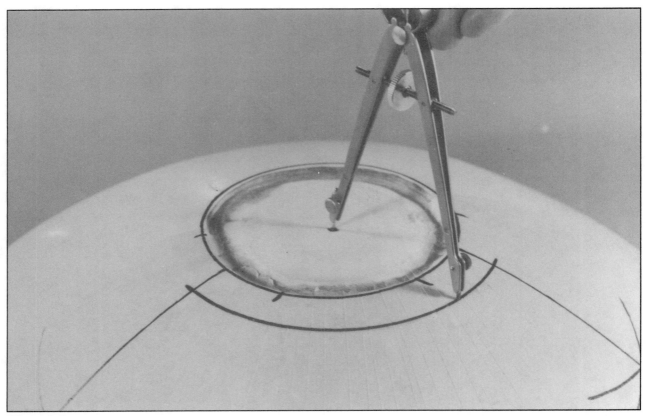

Photo 9.7

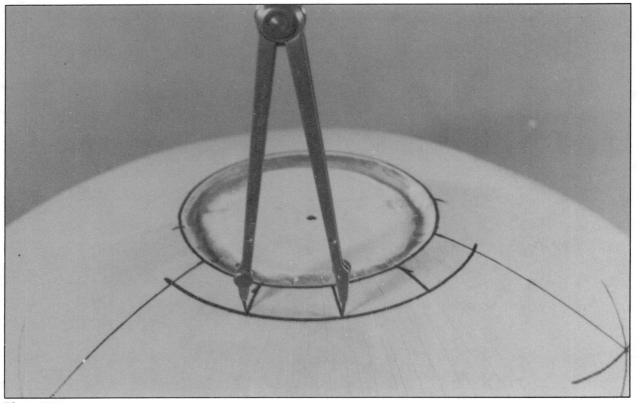

Photo 9.8

Creating A Repeating Design

One of the most effective design techniques used in lampmaking is repeating a design around the mold. Repeats create the illusion of a complete pattern without actually designing over the entire form. Each repeat appears in exactly the same position on the mold, so they also balance the composition.

You can produce another special effect by changing the color scheme of primary design elements from one return to another. By treating each return as a separate color composition, variations in flowers, leaves, and other elements will create visual interest and appear as a non-repeating scheme.

Creating the return is a matter of transferring the left edge of the design over to the right side and joining the linear design elements at the juncture. It is therefore necessary to allow the left vertical boundary to appear behind, or through the design, as I instructed in Step 2, above. This "keyline" will be used to position the left design section over the right vertical boundary line. For the next procedure you will need the following for this stage:

- Two single-edge razor blades
- An X-acto blade or a straight pin
- A fine-tip permanent marker
- Sheet of clear acetate

The two single-edge razor blades will be used to cut out a heartline between the design's pattern pieces. They will be taped together so that their blades are spaced slightly apart and positioned parallel to each other. Take a small piece of matchbook cover or very thin cardboard and place it between the two blades. Position the blades upside down on a table top, with the cardboard between them. When the blades are squeezed together, the space between the two blades should be no more than $\frac{1}{16}$". Add or remove spacers to get as close to this measurement as possible. When you are satisfied with

the position and spacing of the blades, wrap their blunt edges with masking tape, joining the two and creating a padded handle. The blades can now be used to cut out the design shapes drawn on the mold's surface (see Photo 9.10).

Procedure

1. Beginning at the top of the design on the left side of the mold, run the corner points of the two razor blades along the pattern lines. Cut out all of the patterns through which the left vertical boundary line passes. As you do this, the blades should create two visible, parallel cuts in the masking tape. The cuts should go completely through the tape (see Photo 9.11).

2. When you are finished, go back and remove the heartline of masking tape from around all of the pattern pieces using an X-acto blade or straight pin. This thin strip should easily lift up, revealing the mold's bare surface underneath (see Photo 9.12).

3. With a fine-tip permanent marker, draw in all of the exposed heartlines. This will transfer the outline of the pieces onto the surface of the mold (see Photo 9.13).

Before removing any patterns from the mold, number and label all of the shapes that now appear on the surface, except those through which the left boundary passes. It is a good practice to label each design element with an identifiable code distinguishing its templates from others. "F" for flowers, "L" for leaves, "B" for background, etc. This will aid in storing the templates and also save time when laying them out in preparation for cutting the glass.

4. Using the X-acto blade or a large straight pin, begin at the top of the design and pry up the upper left corner of the top-most pattern piece with the vertical bound-

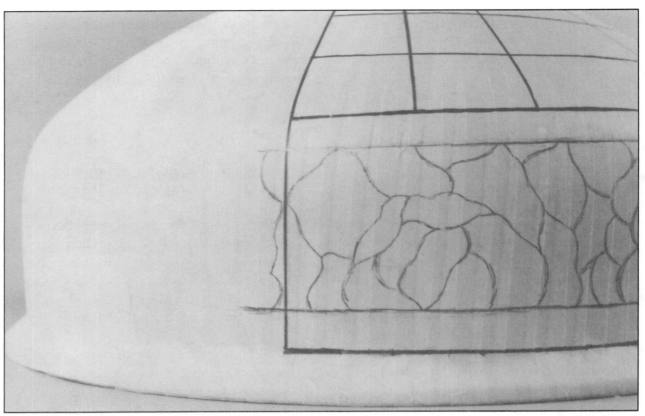

Photo 9.9

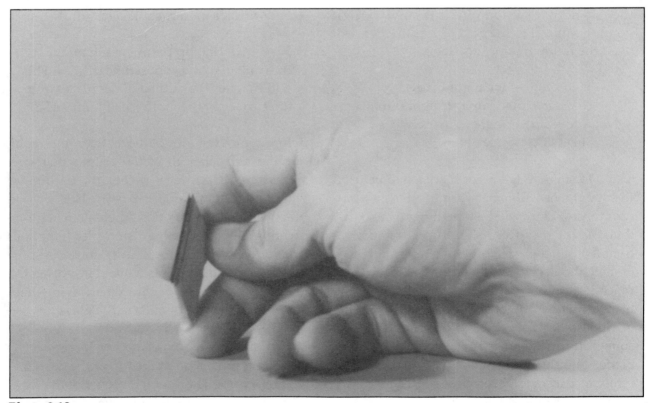

Photo 9.10

Photo 9.11

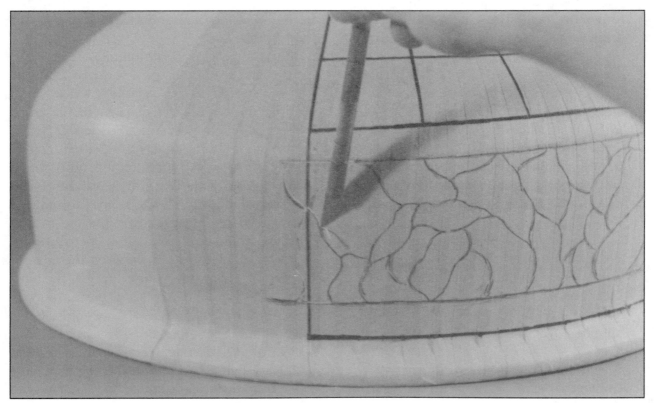

Photo 9.12

THE LAMPMAKING HANDBOOK

ary line passing through it. Pull up enough of the pattern to grasp it between your fingers and remove the entire piece. Pull from left to right. If the masking tape was correctly applied in an overlapping sequence from left to right, the entire pattern piece should lift easily from the surface (see Photo 9.14). As the pattern piece is removed, write the corresponding pattern number on the blank space.

5. Take the pattern piece to the opposite (right) side of the design. Lay it on the mold in the same position it occupied on the left side of the design, using the right vertical boundary line as a guide. Place the pattern so that the straight line running through it (the former left vertical boundary) and the right boundary line, are aligned (see Photo 9.15).

6. Proceed to the next pattern piece (the one directly under the first). Continue down the line until all of the pieces have been transferred to the right side of the design. Remember to allow $\frac{1}{16}$" space between pattern pieces when transferring from left to right. This space represents the heartline removed when the patterns were cut out (see Photo 9.16).

7. When you have completed the transfer, draw around all of the repositioned pattern pieces with a fine-tip permanent marker.

8. You can now remove the original patterns from the right side of the mold and apply them to a pattern material, such as clear acetate, to cut out working templates. The adhesive on the back of the tape should still be sticky.

9. Cut out the heartlines of the newly drawn shapes and remove the pieces from the mold. They are only duplicates of the originals, so they can be discarded.

The design has now been set up to repeat from one section of the mold to its adjoining section. The line of pattern pieces sharing the vertical boundaries occupies the same position on either side; they are "repeated" on the left and right. All that remains, before removing the rest of the patterns from the surface, is to complete any design details left in the blank areas to the left of the right return and number any pieces that remain (see Photo 9.17).

Remove the remaining pattern pieces from the surface of the mold in small groups of about five or six pieces at a time. This avoids any confusion during the process. Remember to number the space on the mold as you lift the pattern piece from it.

When transferring the masking tape pattern to a template material (clear or frosted acetate), be sure that the template sits flat and does not buckle up, distorting the shape. Press the pieces firmly onto the template material. Keep all pattern sheets together and label them with the name of the lamp.

Cut out templates with regular scissors. Because each pattern shape is isolated from the rest, it is not necessary to remove a heart from around the template. Cut right to the edge, being careful not to cut into the shape.

As you free the templates, check them against their corresponding space on the mold. When held against the design, you should be able to see the pattern outline (black line) around the template. If the template covers the line, it is too big and should be trimmed (see Photo 9.18).

If blank space appears between the edge of the template and the pattern outline the template is too small. Undersized pieces of glass will result in thick and unsightly solder lines. They should, therefore, be re-created. Position a clear piece of acetate over the pattern outline and trace the shape onto it. Cut the new template from the acetate, and check it against the design mold for accuracy.

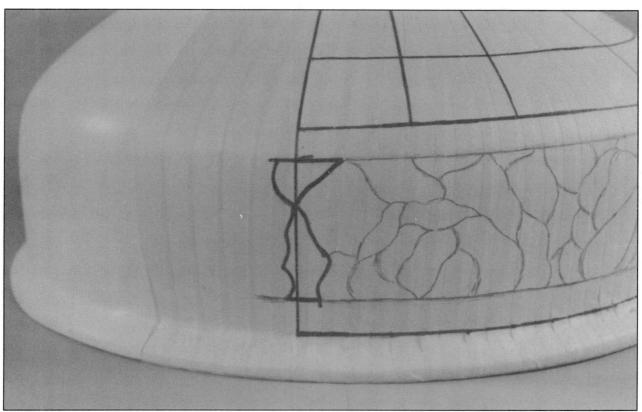

Photo 9.13

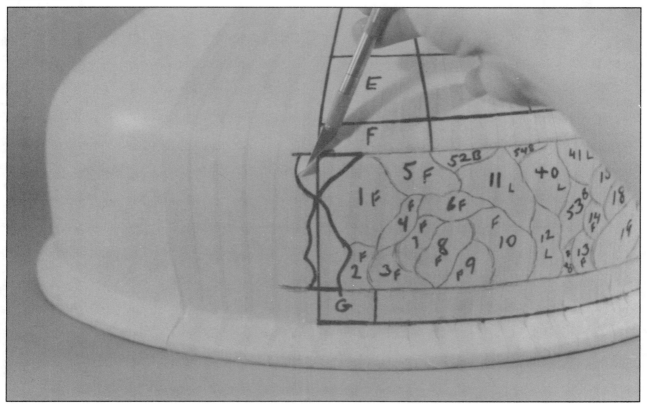

Photo 9.14

THE LAMPMAKING HANDBOOK

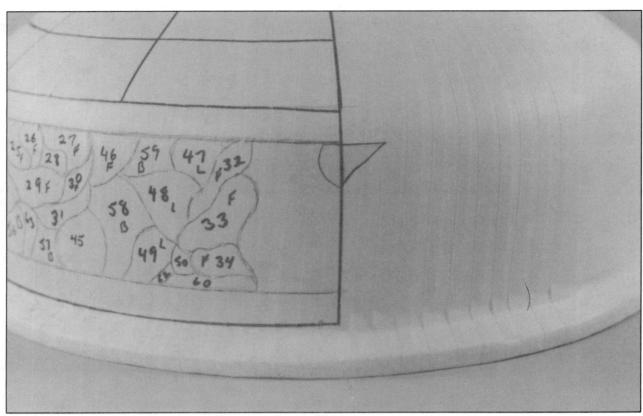

Photo 9.15

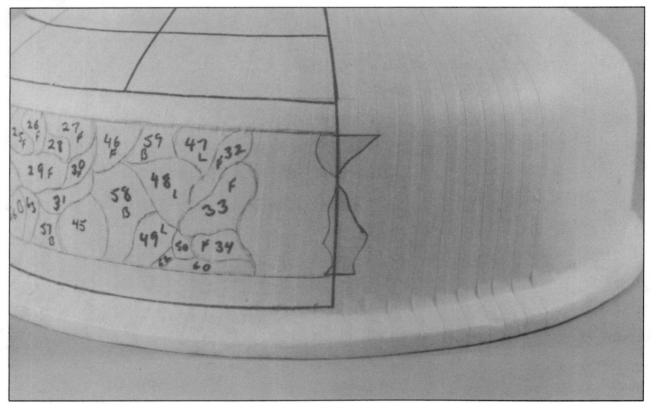

Photo 9.16

Keep patterns for specific design elements in separate groups (i.e., flowers, stems and background). Store these templates in envelopes labelled with the name of the lamp and the enclosed pattern group. Keep the envelopes for an entire lamp in one resealable plastic bag. Stored this way, any template pieces that escape from individual envelopes will not be lost. Keeping these pieces from becoming misplaced is of paramount importance.

Creating A Master Layout

A master layout is needed before you can begin cutting glass from your new templates. Place a blank sheet of clear plastic acetate over the design on the mold. Trace the design onto the acetate with a fine-tip permanent marker (secure the sheet of acetate to the mold with masking tape before you begin). Working down the surface of the mold, trace outlines and pattern numbers onto the clear sheet. Be sure to trace all pattern shapes onto the layout sheet.

Be aware that tracing from a curved surface onto a flat one will result in small amounts of distortion. This will cause the design to spread in some areas, creating spaces between pattern pieces. These spaces must be blackened in, to avoid any confusion when laying out templates (see Photo 9.19).

Absolute accuracy is not necessary in the master layout. We have already guaranteed the accuracy of our templates to the design on the mold and do not need such accuracy in our master layout. It will function only as a reference for positioning our glass pieces during cutting. Label the master layout with the name of the lamp design and a key describing the codes used for the different pattern groups.

Tape the master to a piece of clear glass or Plexiglass. This protects it from damage and makes it easier to store. It also provides a flat, smooth surface to cut on, and makes moving the cut glass pieces (once they've been placed on the layout) easy. You are now ready to begin

the actual lamp construction (see Photo 9.20).

Choosing Colors

A well-selected palette of colors and glass textures greatly enhances any lamp design. Many color decisions can be made even before any glass is pulled from the rack.

A design scheme is broken down into its major design elements of background, foreground and border (if any). Each should be considered separately and then judged against the others. When considering color possibilities, ask the following questions before selecting your glass. These will narrow the many choices and might suggest alternatives that would otherwise be overlooked:

- What function will the glass color perform? Will it support the surrounding glasses? Will it work with the surrounding glass in an arrangement of tonal relationships, such as a grouping of flower petals whose inner areas grow deeper in tone, and whose extreme areas are lighter? Will it stand alone in contrast to its surroundings, such as green leaves set against red to enhance the intensity of the scheme? Or will the color be used to convey a certain feeling or attitude, as might be the case in strictly geometric or abstract designs?

- Will glass texture be necessary to achieve any special effects, such as an undulating flower petal or a rippled flower center? If a border exists, can a textured glass be introduced that will not compete with other elements in the design? Will textured glass be used in other parts of the lamp? Will a textured border result in overkill?

- Can any special coloring effects be considered? Will a transitional back-

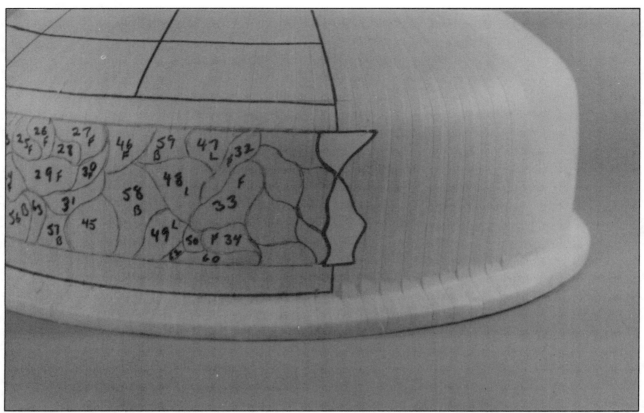

Photo 9.17

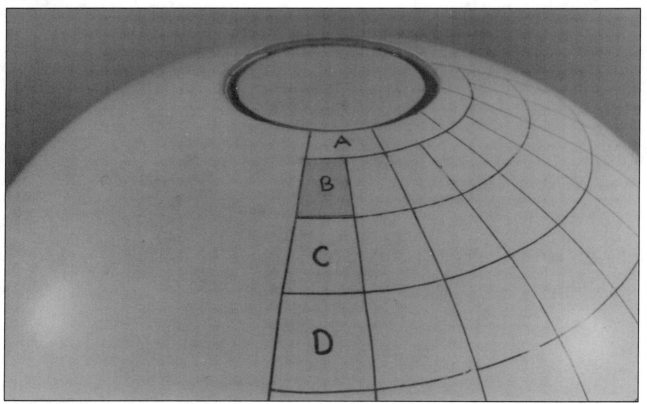

Photo 9.18

ground, one whose colors change from the top to the bottom of the shade, add to the beauty of the lamp? Can a setting sun or varied landscape be suggested using this technique? Can floral designs be enhanced by multi-colored glasses that introduce other tones either on the interior or exterior edges of the individual floral elements (petals)? Can a specific season be portrayed by choosing certain colors? Can the design profit from an overall color treatment where each return of the design uses a separate color scheme?

- Can a specific glass type, such as mottled or streaky, achieve or enhance a given effect (such as dappled sunlight, sky or water)?

- How have similar designs and color schemes been handled by other artists or in other media, such as painting, interior design, etc? Can their approach to color be translated into glass?

- Can the choice of colors be narrowed to the smallest possible number?

- Do the choices work well together aesthetically?

Not all of these must be considered for every project, but familiarity with these questions will help make the final choice of colors an intelligent one, based on solid criteria rather than haphazard trial-and-error.

Very few artists and craftspeople are born with an acute sense of color coordination. It is an ability that develops through practice and testing, and it is a continual learning process. Many artists shy away from selecting colors, feeling insecure in their choices because they lack training or what they describe as an "eye" for color. Training will teach you a great deal

about color, but it cannot make the choices for you. Any amount of instruction will still leave you on your own to make the selections.

Glass artists learn to trust their eyes, if only because light activated colored glass creates its own rules concerning hue, value and intensity. To better judge art glass, let us define hue, value and intensity as they relate to lampmaking.

Hue

Hue and color are synonymous in lampmaking. Blue, yellow, brown are all hues. Hue is simply the name of the color.

Value

Value is a judgement made against a color's relation to white or black. The closer a color is to white, the higher its value. The closer it is to black, the lower its value. In other words, the lightness or darkness of a color distinguishes its value. Values can be judged against colors of the same family. For instance, a light sky-blue has a higher value than a deep, royal-blue. A bright lemon-yellow has a higher value than a mustard amber-yellow. On the other hand, a deep ruby-red has a lower value than an orange-red, which will appear brighter, and a forest green has a lower value than a yellowish-green. Grasping the concept of value in color not only helps distinguish light colors from dark, it also aids in choosing between the more subtle gradations found in single color groups.

Intensity

The strength of a color is its intensity. The amount of uncompromising color determines its intensity or saturation. These terms are also interchangeable. A solid blue is more intense than the same color tempered with white. A green streaked with yellow will be less intense than the same green in its pure state.

Warm And Cool Colors

Although relatively easy to understand, the

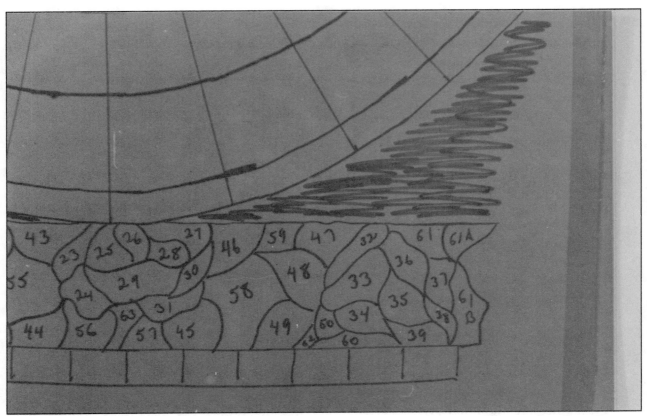

Photo 9.19

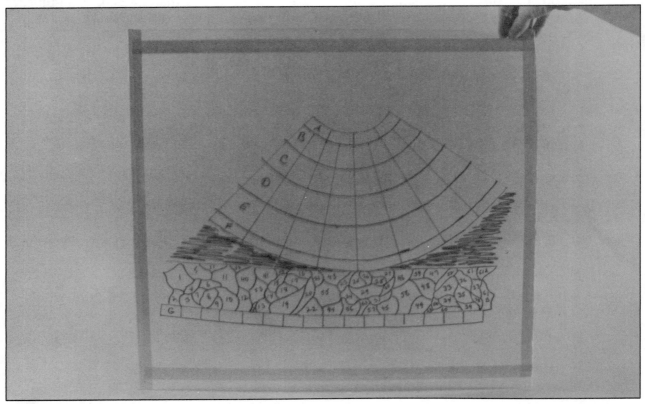

Photo 9.20

concept of warm and cool colors is evasive until clarified. Reds, oranges and yellows are considered warm colors because they remind us of heat and light. Greens and blues remind us of land, sea and ice, and are considered cool. Warm colors seem to come forward, while cool colors recede. This is as true with colored glass as it is with painting. Warm or hot colors will jump out of a color scheme, catching the eye and, in extreme cases, distracting from other colors in the composition. Cool colors will soothe and, when properly used, will provide strong support to the design.

Depth and spatial relationships can be achieved using these properties. Impressionists painters added blue to elements they wished to recede, while introducing warmer tones to those elements occupying the foreground. In lamps, these same techniques can be used to designate primary and secondary elements of a design, or to have backgrounds recede from the primary imagery.

When applying these color qualities to glass, the addition of light affects three of the four categories. Hue, value and intensity all change when viewing a piece of glass from reflected to transmitted light. Most times, light will lighten the glass' hues and make its value higher, but lessen glass intensity (depending upon what has been added to the base color). Different amounts of light will produce subtle changes in glass. Small amounts of light will gently activate subordinate colorings, creating a dramatic effect, especially on hand-rolled varieties. Most colored glasses react best to minimal amounts of transmitted light.

Some mottled glasses actually look darker, or lose intensity under transmitted light. This is due to the higher concentration of colors beneath the surface. The area or ring-and-pin mottling hidden beneath the surface of the glass act as little shades, or blinders, blocking light as it attempts to pass through. A similar effect can be produced by holding a piece of non-mottled glass up to the light and placing the tip of your finger behind it. Although the hue and value of the pure-colored areas might be heightened, the intensity of the mottled sections, the degree of which is determined by the saturation of mottling, will be less. This property makes mottled glass an excellent option for shading and creating depth or perspective.

Textured glass shares the same property but to a lesser extent, as the thickness of the textured areas will govern the amount and quality of light that passes through. Where the mass of material is greatest, less light will be allowed through, causing what looked like brilliant color to appear shaded. Given the tightness of most textured surfaces, this quality brings about the dappled look that, aside from the tactile attraction of the glass surface, is so desirable in these glasses.

Increasing amounts of illumination, especially incandescent, add brilliance to most colors. If carried to extremes, though, excessive illumination will wash colors out. Hot spots, created by light bulbs of unnecessarily high wattage, rob glass closest to the light source of most of its color effect, leaving in its wake distracting areas of illumination. Avoid such situations by striving for the least amount of illumination (bulb strength) needed to light the work.

The study of glass color in its many facets and subtleties is a lifelong pursuit. New advancements in glass technology and production keep the field of color psychology ever active.

The key to staying in touch with your developing color sense is to constantly weigh your color selections against your own sensitivities, no matter how experienced you may feel about them, and to be aware of the reactions of others to your selections. Take the lessons learned from your last work into your latest work.

Study the use of color and glass in other works. The Tiffany Studios' lamps and windows offer a wealth of information about glass selection and color schemes. Many books are available on Tiffany's works (consult the bibliography). Take special note of how Tiffany's glass artists composed their color, using density and mottling to suggest shade and depth. They used textured glass to introduce a three-dimensional quality to certain elements in a design. Transitional backgrounds from light to dark and from one color to another add a spectacular effect to some lamps while creating a subtle color exchange in others. Border glasses pick up colors used in the primary scheme, bringing that color forward. Individual flower petals of multi-colored glass are composed with high concentrations of color on the innermost petal sections, suggesting depth through color rather than shading. Colors of primary images appear in surrounding elements such as backgrounds, borders and other areas, and vice versa.

Nature can also be a great teacher when studying or exploring color relationships to be translated into glass. Not all study of nature needs to take place in the garden or outdoors. Photographs and books are again the most versatile and convenient sources, offering the widest array of visual information at the turn of a page. Armed with the encyclopedia of color possibilities that these sources offer, guesswork can be avoided and intelligent choices based on real experience and skills will rescue works from the threat of mediocrity. ■

10

The Past Present and Future of Lampmaking

The stained glass lamp is a uniquely American art form. It is not the result of an Americanization of a European precedent, as is the case with leaded glass windows, blown glass and other artistic and decorative glassworking techniques. Nor was its development a rediscovery of a lost craft. Little more than 100 years ago, there was no such thing as the stained glass lamp. It just did not exist.

Its early development is shrouded in mystery. No definitive evidence links its beginnings to one person or studio. It is understood that the Tiffany Studios did not invent the crafting of stained glass lamps, but embraced the art form as a vehicle to further promote its revolutionary art glass and glass design aesthetic. In doing so, and as a result of Tiffany's great success in promoting his firm's works, the Tiffany lamp enjoyed success almost to the exclusion of other lamps made by contemporaries of Tiffany. Lampmakers such as Handel & Co., Duffner and Kimberly, Bigelow-Kennard & Co. and Bradley & Hubbard also produced stained glass shades, some approaching Tiffany's in beauty and quality. Yet their accomplishments were overshadowed by the overwhelming suc-

cess and popularity of those of the Tiffany Studios. The Tiffany lamp became a generic term for any lampshade made of stained glass, regardless of the manufacturer.

It is interesting to note that most of the major manufacturers of stained glass lamps of that time were located in the northeast section of the country. This reinforces the belief that the form had its origins there.

It is also interesting that even the earliest examples of stained glass lamps, whether still in existence or documented by illustration in old sales catalogs, represent an art form that is already well developed. There are few examples of crude, early stained glass lamps. There seems to be no gradual development of the form. In the recent attempts to record the short history of this American phenomenon, little evidence has come to light to aid in the search for its origins. The stained glass lamp surfaces during the late 19th century in its current form. The crafting methods and aesthetics applied to the earliest lamps are still employed today. Although technology has improved some of the tools and related techniques, stained glass lamps are still being designed and built the same way. In a quirk of decorative art history, a form and its fundamental methods of construction emerges from nowhere it seems, full blown, with little need for improvement save for those related to developing materials, technology and improved working equipment.

Most of the earliest documented lamps display more invention and experimentation than those that followed. The Tiffany Spider Webs, for example, the rarest and most valuable of the firm's creations, were created during the firm's early experiments with the form, before the turn of the century. In the Spider Web, we see a flair of invention unmatched by Tiffany's contemporaries and unique within his own oeuvre, as well. These masterpieces display a iron grasp of the concepts guiding artificially illuminated colored glass fixed into an autonomous sculptural form. The level of craftsmanship (in both glassmaking and metalworking) that they display is astounding. The successful integration of stained glass and metal is remarkable and difficult to reproduce, even with the technological advances made over the last century. The Spider Web is as awe-inspiring today as it must have been when it was first created.

Stained glass lamps were products of an in-dustrial environment. That is to say, each step in the creation of the work was executed by an artisan whose talents and abilities were specific to that process. The production of a stained glass lamp was departmentalized The product of many rather than the efforts of one.

The work done in the context of originality and imagination propels a medium from stagnation and mediocrity into new and exciting environments of expression and acceptance. It is my hope that the information contained in this book, and the conscientious application of that information, will inspire more artists and craftspeople to consider the stained glass lamp as a means of personal expression through glass. It was that kind of energy that nurtured the craft during the early part of the 20th century, the period that saw the stained glass lamp develop and become a popular decorative, and in some cases, fine art. Given the health and vitality of the contemporary glass community, the time is right for a renaissance of sorts, a renaissance that will re-establish the stained glass lamp, long the bastard child of American art glass, as an accessible and fertile autonomous glass art form, rich in its short tradition, casting a bright light into the future. ■

11

Health And Safety In Lampmaking

by Monona Rossol, M.S., M.F.A., Industrial Hygienist

Health and safety laws and regulations affect almost every aspect of our work. Most of us know little about these laws and feel that somehow they don't really apply to us. They do. We must educate ourselves if we are to work in the real world.

Businesses And OSHA

If you are an employer or an employee in a glass studio, conditions in the shop are regulated by the Occupational Health and Safety Administration (OSHA). The legislative act empowering OSHA begins with a general duty clause which reads in part "every employer shall furnish employment and a place of employment which are free from recognized hazards . . ."

This brief statement serves as the foundation for a vast number of rules about lead and other chemical exposures, noise, machinery guarding, and a host of subjects. If you do not have a copy of these regulations, call your nearest de-partment of labor and ask for the occupational safety and health general industry standards (29 Code of Federal regulations 1900-1910). Although they are not reader-friendly, become as familiar with them as possible.

If employers do not learn about the rules and train their employees about them willingly, OSHA, and sometimes the courts, can force them to. This enforcement is necessary and beneficial. Despite the bitter complaints we hear about restrictive OSHA rules and excessive jury awards, enforcement works. Word of mouth reporting of one inspection, citation, or lawsuit has been observed to improve safety practices in an entire county overnight.

The Right-To-Know

Certain recently instituted regulations are proving particularly useful in pressing us to upgrade our health and safety practices. These are the so-called "Right-To-Know" laws. Right-to-know laws were first passed by a number of individual states. A similar federal regulation called the OSHA Hazard Communication Standard (HAZCOM) was then instituted. The result is that almost all employees in the United States are now covered by one or the other (sometimes both) of these laws. Even federal workers, so long exempt from OSHA regulations, come under this rule.

Essentially, all employees in the United States are covered by state or federal hazard communication (right-to-know) laws. A few employers in states that do not have an accepted state OSHA plan are still exempt. Often these exempted employers find they must comply anyway or jeopardize their insurance coverage because the right-to-know is a nationally accepted standard of safety practice.

All employers in workplaces where hazardous materials are present, therefore, are required to develop these type of programs and train their employees. (The employer is the person or entity that takes deductions out of employee paychecks.)

Self-Employed or Hobby Glass Artist

As a self-employed artist, teacher or hobbyist, you are not covered by OSHA. You are allowed to harm yourself without interference. However, you may be affected by the right-to-know laws. For example, if you work as an independent contractor working or teaching at a site where there are employees, all the products and materials you bring onto the premises must conform to the employer's right-to-know program labeling requirements. Your use of these products must also conform.

Teachers

Teachers have a unique right-to-know obligation arising from the fact that they can be held legally liable for any harm classroom activities cause their students. To protect their liability, teachers must formally transmit to students right-to-know training about the dangers of classroom materials and processes. They must also enforce the safety rules and practice good safety precautions to present useful examples.

Running Your Right-To-Know Program

Once right-to-know programs are in place, it is usually not difficult or expensive to maintain them. The hard part is facing the fact that we must make some basic changes in the way we work and teach. It is well worth the effort. In addition, the right-to-know laws are creating a much-needed uniform and professional system of chemical awareness, storage and handling in education and the crafts.

To comply, first find out whether you come under a state or federal right-to-know law. Call your local department of labor and ask them which law affects you and where to obtain a copy of the law. Also ask for any available explanatory materials. Some of the government agencies have prepared well written guidelines to take you through compliance step by step. In general, the laws require employers to:

1. Institute hazard communication programs (often these programs must include a formally written plan).

2. Inventory all workplace chemicals. Even products such as bleach and cleaning materials may qualify as hazardous products. List everything. (This is an excellent time to cut down paperwork by trimming inventory. Dispose of old, unneeded or seldom-used products.)

3. Identify hazardous products in your inventory. (Apply the definition of "hazardous" from the right-to-know law which applies to you. Even better, consider all products to be hazardous and go to step four. Often so called "nonhazardous" consumer products may be hazardous if are used in amounts or in ways which ordinary consumers would not use them.)

4. Assemble Material Safety Data Sheets (MSDSs) on all hazardous products. MSDSs are technical health and safety information documents. Write to manufacturers, distributors, and importers of all products on hand for MSDSs. Require MSDSs as a condition of purchase for all new materials.

5. Check all product labels to be sure they comply with the law's labeling requirements. Products which do not comply must be relabeled or discarded.

6. Prepare and apply proper labels to all containers into which chemicals have been transferred. (Chemicals in unlabeled containers that are used up within one shift need not be labeled.) Rules for the types of information and warning symbols which conform to your right-to-know law can be obtained from your local labor department.

7. Consult Material Safety Data Sheets to identify all operations which use or generate hazardous materials. Be aware that nonhazardous materials when chemically reacted, heated, or burned may produce toxic emissions which come under the law.

8. Make all lists of hazardous materials, Material Safety Data Sheets, reports, and other required written materials available to employees.

9. Implement a training program for all employees who may be potentially exposed to toxic chemicals.

Training

Many employers and workers alike find the training provision of the right-to-know laws the hardest to swallow. They can't believe that OSHA really expects each worker to be trained to understand basic toxicology, risk assessment, and exposure standards in lay terms. But OSHA does.

OSHA's rationale is that it makes no sense to provide workers with Material Safety Data Sheets if they cannot understand them. OSHA wants workers to understand concepts such as:

* Flash point, evaporation rate, and other physical data and the meaning of toxic
* Routes of exposure (skin contact, inhalation and ingestions)
* Differences between acute and chronic illnesses
* Cumulative versus non-cumulative toxins
* Sensitizers (chemicals which cause allergy)
* Carcinogens, mutagens (causes mutations), and teratogens (causes birth defects)
* Threshold Limit Values, Permissible Exposure Limits and other air quality standards

If these concepts, as well as many others, are not understood by workers who use toxic substances, their employer is in violation of the right-to-know training requirement. This chapter and some of the reading material listed in the Bibliography can be used for proper training.

Air Contaminants

Lampmaking processes often release toxic substances into the air. To understand the hazards of these substances, right-to-know programs must cover the following definitions of gases, vapors, fumes, dusts, mists and smoke.

Gases: We can picture gases as many molecules moving rapidly and randomly in space. Gases vary greatly in toxicity. They can be irritating, acidic, caustic, poisonous, and so on. Some gases also have dangerous physical properties such as flammability or reactivity. Examples would be highly toxic hydrogen sulfide (rotten egg odor) created by some patinas, or flammable propane gas used as a propellant in some spray can products.

Some gases are not toxic. An inert gas such as carbon dioxide used to carbonate beverages is an example. Such gases are dangerous only when present in such large quantities that they reduce the amount of oxygen in the air to levels insufficient to support life. In this case, these are called "asphyxiants."

Vapors: Toxic vapors created in stained glass include organic chemical vapors from solvents such as alcohol and turpentine. Vapors, like gases, may vary greatly in toxicity, flammability and reactivity.

Vapors are the gaseous form of liquids. For example, water vapor is created when water evaporates, that is, releases vapor molecules into the air. Once released into the air, vapors behave like gases and expand into space. However, at high concentrations they will re-condense into liquids. This is what happens when it rains. Other vapors also will re-condense at high concentrations.

Particulates: Unlike gases and vapors which are molecules, particulates are aggregates of many molecules. Particulates include fumes, dusts and mists.

Fumes: Very tiny particles usually created when metals are heated in operations such as soldering. They form when hot metal vapors cool rapidly and condense into fine particles.

Fume particles are so small that they tend to remain airborne for long periods of time. Eventually, however, they will settle to contaminate dust in the workplace, in the ventilation ducts, in your hair or clothing, or wherever air currents carry them. This is why OSHA requires that all workers shower and change clothes before leaving workplaces where lead is used. Lead workers have been known to carry

enough fume home on shoes and clothing to harm family members, especially children. The toxicity of lead fume also prompted the Centers for Disease Control in their 1985 guidelines on prevention of lead toxicity in children to specifically mention the risk to children when stained glass work is done in the home.

Although fume particles are too small to be seen by the naked eye, they can sometimes be perceived as a bluish haze rising like cigarette smoke from soldering operations. Fuming tends to increase the toxicity of a substance because the small particle size enables it to be inhaled deeply into the lungs.

Dusts: Dusts are formed when solid materials are broken down into small particles by either natural or mechanical forces. Grinding or sanding are examples of forces which produce dusts. Powdered chemicals also contain dust.

Large dust particles may cause irritation or allergy symptoms in the nose, throat and eyes. The finer dusts, called "respirable dusts," are inhaled deeper into the lungs and may cause respiratory problems. Respirable dusts are too small to be seen with the naked eye. Most powdered chemicals and grinding dust will contain both visible and respirable dust particles.

Mists: Any liquid, water, oil, or solvent, can be misted or aerosolized. The finer these mist droplets, the more deeply the mist can be inhaled and the more likely it is to harm delicate lung tissue.

Some mists, such as spray-can mists or the water mists created during wet grinding and polishing, also contain solid material. These mists can float on air currents for a time. The liquid portion of the droplet will then vaporize—convert to a vapor—and the solid part of the mist will settle as a dust. If the mist is created from abrading lead glass, the solid component is also a source of lead exposure.

Smoke: Smoke is formed from burning organic

matter. Burning wood and hot wire-cutting of plastics are two smoke-producing activities. Smoke is usually a mixture of many gases, vapors, and fumes. For example, cigarette smoke contains over four thousand chemicals, including carbon monoxide gas, benzene vapor, and fume-sized particles of tar.

Exposure Standards

Exposure to airborne chemicals in the workplace is regulated in the United States by OSHA. OSHA's standards are called Permissible Exposure Limits (PELs). Permissible Exposure Limits are based on standards called Threshold Limit Value (TLV). The permissible Exposure Limits for most substances are identical to their Threshold Limit Values. Where there is a difference it is usually brought about by the political influence of industry.

For more complete information about TLVs and PELS, see some of the references in the Bibliography. OSHA requires that workers understand this material so that they can use it to identify which substances are most hazardous. In general, the smaller the Threshold Limit Value or Permissible Exposure Limit, the more toxic the substance (see Table 1).

TABLE 1
WORKPLACE AIR QUALITY STANDARDS

Represented here as Threshold Limit Values (TLV) or Permissible Exposure Limits (PELS), whichever is most protective:

Aluminum
aluminum metal 10
(milligrams/cubic meter)
aluminum oxide abrasive 10
aluminum fume 5
Zinc
zinc oxide dust 10
zinc metal fume 5

zinc chloride fume from flux 1
Tin
metal, oxide and compounds 2

Antimony
metal and compounds 0.5

Lead
metal dust, fume, compounds . . . 0.05

The OSHA Lead Standard

If lead is used in a business, the employer almost always must comply with the OSHA Lead Standard. The standard requires initial monitoring of exposed employees to see if they are exposed to lead above a certain amount (the standard's action level). If the action level is exceeded, employers will have to meet many expensive requirements: regular blood tests for employees, record-keeping, air sampling, providing showers and changing rooms, and more.

It is very important not to avoid compliance with this law—not only to avoid severe penalties, but to keep workers and their children healthy. The effects of lead are so subtle and long lasting that generations of a family can be adversely affected.

The hazards of lead and the OSHA Lead Standard are two very good reasons to take the extra time to master the use of lead-free solders. Fortunately, new lead-free solders originally developed for plumbing water pipes will work for stained glass purposes. In addition, it is likely that lead-free solders will be modified and improved in the near future. Many solder manufacturers already make solders that work well for stained glass purposes.

Lead-free solders appropriate for stained glass work are made of silver, tin, copper, and zinc. Some lead-free solders contain antimony. These are too toxic. Lead- and antimony-free solders cost about twice what lead solders cost, but they are cheaper than the cost of meeting the lead laws. Again, always refer to a product's MSDS for ingredients.

Choosing The Safest Materials

Good training and use of Material Safety Data Sheet information should enable stained glass artists to choose the safest materials for the job. Some general information about the types of materials often used in lampmaking include the following:

Fluxes: Fluxes are very complex mixtures of chemicals. Many types of chlorides, fluorides, and borates may be found in fluxes. Those containing chlorides, such as zinc chloride, are skin, eye, and respiratory irritants. Fluoride fluxes are even more irritating and can cause lung damage and long-term systemic damage to bones and teeth. Boric acid and borate fluxes are only moderately toxic and irritating and are safest to use. Most fluxes contain some organic materials as well, such as oleic acid and other fatty acids. These are not toxic, but decompose to emit toxic smoke. Rosin fluxes are rarely used in stained glass work, but they can cause allergies and asthma.

Fluoride fluxes should be avoided if possible. All fluxing processes require ventilation. Respiratory protection may not be sufficient. Consult product MSDS.

Metal Cleaner: Lead surfaces must be scrupulously clean to be coated with metal or patina. Some of these metal cleaners contain strong caustics, strong acids, chemicals which release hydrofluoric acid, or solvents. Read Materials Safety Data Sheets on these products and follow the precautions suggested on them.

Patinas: Once the surface is prepared the patina can be applied. Patinas are generally of two types: 1) those which react with the metal surface to form metal compounds such as sulfides or oxides, and 2) those which dissolve metal

from the metal surface and replace it with a different metal deposited from the patina chemicals. Both types are composed of chemicals of varying toxicity and they usually produce toxic gases or vapors during application.

Common patina chemicals include copper sulfate and acid solutions. Some of these are strongly acidic and can cause skin and eye damage on contact. They also may give off respiratory- and eye-irritating acid vapors and sulfur dioxide during use.

Selenium-containing patinas may give off highly toxic hydrogen selenide gas during use. Patinas containing highly toxic antimony sulfide may give off both stibene gas and hydrogen sulfide. Avoid patinas containing antimony or sulfides when possible, and use good ventilation with all patinas.

Planning A Safe Studio

Plan studios and shops with health and safety in mind. The studio must be completely isolated and separated from living areas. This is especially imperative if lead is used. Never allow children into areas where lead or other toxic chemicals are used. If the studio comes under the OSHA Lead Standard, you may have to install showers, changing rooms, and other safety related features.

Plan for easy maintenance. Floors and surfaces should be made of materials which are easily sponged and mopped clean. Be prepared to clean up or contain spills. Enough space should be allowed around equipment for maneuvering during cleaning. Follow Material Safety Data Sheet advice and order materials for spill control and chemical disposal.

Plan and install ventilation systems appropriate for the work to be done. Provide general ventilation, heating, and air-conditioning sufficient to keep people comfortable throughout the studio (see Illus. 11.1). In addition, provide some type of local exhaust, such as slot vents, flexible duct systems, or a window exhaust fan at worktable level (see Illus. 11.2-4). Use local exhaust for all operations involving soldering, tinning, dry cleaning (with whiting), or polishing, applying patinas or any other operation which produces toxic emissions or dust.

Install proper fire extinguishers (ABC type) and post and practice fire evacuation procedures. Users of the studio should have a short hands-on training session with fire extinguishers so they will know how to use them. It is too late to read the directions when smoke is curling about your head.

Design the studio for maximum separation of wet and dry processes. Keep ordinary electrical equipment and outlets separated from wet grinding areas where they may splash water or mists are produced. Install ground fault interrupters (GFIs) or circuit breakers which will cut off current to faulty equipment immediately.

Plan for comfort breaks. Eating, drinking, smoking, applying makeup and other personal hygiene tasks should not be done in the studio. Eating, recreating, and bathroom facilities should be in separate rooms or a short distance from the studio. This practice is not just for studios using lead, but should be followed whenever any toxic material is used.

Safe Equipment
Grinders: Only purchase equipment that meets

standards for safety and health. Stationary grind wheels must be equipped with a built-in local exhaust ventilation system and face guards. Wet grinding, polishing and cutting wheels should also have face guards. Wet grinding equipment should be cleaned when wet to avoid dust exposure. Remember, dust from grinding lead glass also can be a source of exposure to lead.

Wet grinders that use running tap water sources are preferred. Those with water reservoirs must be cleaned often to remove scum or

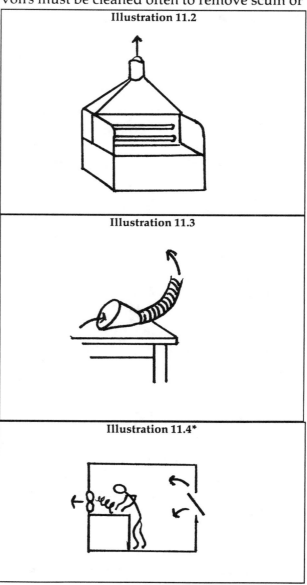

Illustration 11.2

Illustration 11.3

Illustration 11.4*

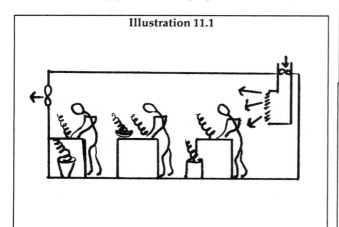

Illustration 11.1

A typical inexpensive dilution system used to reduce workers' exposure to small amounts of moderately toxic gases or vapors from many point sources.

*Many municipal codes do not allow the use of this system. Check local regulations.

other microbe growth. Respiratory infections, even Legionnaires Disease, are associated with inhalation of mists of stagnant water from such sources. This type of hazard is invisible.

Asbestos or ceramic fiber board tabletops, gloves and other insulated materials are hazards. These should be replaced with refractory brick materials and other fiber-free substitutes.

Cleaning Equipment: Clean the studio by methods which do not raise dust. The best and cheapest method is wet mopping. Sweeping, even with sweeping compound, is not recommended. Never use shop vacuums, household vacuums, or vacuums which pass dust through a water reservoir in the machine. These vacuums allow fine respirable dusts to pass through them and back into the studio air. Proper vacuums are HEPA (high efficiency particulate air) types available from safety supply and asbestos abatement supply companies.

A proper studio is almost spotless. Clean surfaces and floors frequently. Clean up shards and scraps often. Dusty surfaces and materials lying on the floor are not only unsightly, they are OSHA housekeeping violations.

Personal Protective Equipment: Check product literature and Material Safety Data Sheets for other recommendations. Many will indicate the need for special gloves, goggles, ventilation, respiratory protection and spill control. Stock this safety equipment before using the product.

Safety goggles should be worn whenever you are working with abrasive equipment or breaking glass. These goggles easily fit over prescription glasses and must meet the American National Standards Institutes standard (ANSI Z87.1-1989) for impact and other criteria.

Chemical resistant gloves have been developed for almost any purpose. They can be purchased in lengths from wrist to shoulder, and from see-through thin to thick. They are also made of many materials: natural rubber, butyl rubber, PVC (poly vinyl chloride), PVA (poly vinyl alcohol), nitrile, neoprene, and more. Each of these types may be made from a latex or solvent mixture. They may also be lined.

None of these gloves works for all chemicals. Certain chemicals will degrade or dissolve some types of gloves. Others will penetrate them—often showing no signs of having done so. Workers wearing these gloves are unaware that the chemicals are penetrating the glove and affecting or subsequently penetrating the skin.

For the chemical products suggested in this book, most brands of nitrile and neoprene gloves will provide protection longest. However, readers should obtain information directly from manufacturers or suppliers about gloves they purchase. Be prepared to provide glove manufacturers with the exact names of the chemicals in the materials you will be using.

For workers who are at special risk for accidents, special "chain mail" types of safety gloves are available from safety supply companies. Broken glass cannot penetrate these gloves.

Wear protective clothing such as a smock or coveralls, apron, shoes and haircovering. Even if the OSHA Lead Standard does not apply, those working directly with any toxic materials should leave their work clothes, hair covering and shoes in the studio, to avoid taking dusts home. Wash clothing frequently and separately from other clothing.

First Aid Supplies

Have a first aid kit handy for cuts and accidents. Order a standard industrial first aid kit and keep it stocked. Check the Material Safety Data Sheets of each product you use for any special first aid treatment required and be sure you have it on hand before using the product. Post emergency procedures and telephone numbers where they can be easily found. Be sure every person using the studio is familiar with them and can respond well in an emergency. ∎

GLOSSARY

Aperture: An opening, usually of small diameter, at the top of a lamp or lamp form.

Art Deco: Style in the decorative arts that followed Art Nouveau. Characterized by stylized geometric shapes and cool, subdued colors or by entirely black and white designs.

Art Nouveau: A popular style, most evident in the decorative arts, that proliferated from the turn of the century until the 1930s. It is characterized by floral forms and sensuous, curvilinear shapes.

Calipers: Measuring and drawing tool used to compare similar widths, diameters and small linear distances during lamp design.

Cap Spun metal, decorative unit affixed to the aperture opening of a lamp, usually perforated to allow the escape of heat from the lit lamp.

Collar: See "Ring".

Compass: Design and drawing tool used to establish sectional measurements on a 360 degree mold and create horizontal lines over a curved surface.

Contour drawing: In lampmaking, the outline drawing of a lamp mold's shape.

Contour: The curved vertical edge of a lamp mold.

Dental Pick: A tool, similar to an ice pick, with a long needle-like point, used to remove templates from the surface of a lamp mold.

Fill Solder: Filling the gaps between copper foiled pieces of glass with molten solder without regard for fine leading. Usually performed to solidify a lamp's structure, allowing removal from the mold.

Finial: Sometimes referred to as a cap, or a small pointed metal casting threaded onto a cap to secure it to the base.

Finish Soldering: Final leading of a work's solder lines.

Flexible Curve: A design and drawing tool, usually made of a rubber-like material, that acts like a ruler, but can be bent to assume a curve.

Hardware: Any metal, apart from solder, that attaches to a lamp structure. Collars, caps, rings, and reinforcement wires, are all considered hardware.

Heartline: A small space between pieces of glass into which solder will flow.

Heat Cap: See "Cap".

Lamp Design: The linear image drawn onto the surface of the lamp mold, or form.

Lamp Form: A solid, three dimensional shape onto which a design is drawn and prepared pieces of foiled glass are assembled together.

Lamp Mold: See "Lamp Form".

Master Layout: A reproduction of the lamp design traced from the lamp mold and drawn onto a flat surface, usually a clear acetate, used to place cut and prepared pieces of glass in their appropriate position before assembly.

Metal Coloring Agents: Patina chemicals and solutions. See Patina Chemicals.

Neoprene: Acid and solvent resistant material.

Nitrile: Acid and solvent resistant material.

Patina Chemicals: Powders and liquids used to accelerate the oxidation of metals.

Patina Solutions: See "Patina Chemicals".

Patina: The result of oxidation on a metal surface, or the artificial creation of such.

Pattern: See "Template".

Perimeter: Length of a line around a figure. In lampmaking, the outermost edge of a drawn outline.

Protractor: Design and drawing tool used to determine sectional measurements on a 360-degree, full-form mold.

Reinforcement: The process of adding support, usually in the form of metal wires, to the network of solder lines making up a lamp structure.

Repeat: That portion of the lamp's design that fills one section of a divided lamp mold surface, and repeats without alteration.

Return: See "Repeat".

Ring: A solid wire, usually about $^5/_{32}$" in diameter, made of brass or copper, spun into a circular shape and used to reinforce the bottom edge of a leaded glass lamp.

Sharpie: Brand name of a fine point permanent marker pen used to draw images on a lamp mold surface.

Sweat Soldering: See "Sweating".

Sweating: A soldering technique whereby a metal of greater mass is joined to one of lesser mass by heating it to a point where it absorbs solder by capillary action.

Tack: A small application of solder temporarily bonding two metal surfaces together.

Template: A perfect, physical representation of one outlined area in the design of a leaded glass lamp.

Wood Turner: A craftsperson skilled in creating large, spun shapes out of wood on a lathe.

Work Triangle: The complex of work bench, grinder station and light table utilized during lampmaking.

Bibliography

Albers, Joseph, *Interaction Of Color*, Yale University Press, 1978. Color theory. Exercises in relational and interactive color. A highly technical text. A description of an experimental way of studying and teaching color.

Amaya, Mario, *Tiffany Glass*, Walker And Co., New York, 1967. The "Little Blue Book" of Tiffany. A collector's guide written in the early days of Tiffany's return to popularity.

Duncan, Alastair, *Tiffany At Auction*, Rizzoli, New York, 1981. An entirely illustrated record of Tiffany works that passed through Christie's auction house during one of the most active collecting periods. An indispensable guide for studying lamp-to-base composition and glass color selection. Includes windows and blown glass.

Duncan, Eidelberg, Harris, *Masterworks Of Louis Comfort Tiffany*, Abrams, New York, 1989. An illustrated catalog of the finest Tiffany exhibit to date, in book form. Includes lamps, windows, mosaics, with insightful commentary by the authors.

Feldstein, Duncan, *The Lamps Of Tiffany Studios*, Abrams, New York, 1983. A large, coffee table picture book of Tiffany lamps. A valuable visual reference guide to color and glass selection and composition for lamp artists.

French, Jenny, *Design For Stained Glass*, Van Nostrand Reinhold, 1983. Although the focus of this book is flat glass design and construction, the book contains some of the earliest illustrated attempts to address full-form lampmaking for craftspeople.

Koch, Robert, *Louis C. Tiffany Glass-Bronzes-Lamps*, Crown Publishers, New York, 1971. A collectors' guide to Tiffany. Includes references to lamps, designers, and metal techniques, including patina, practiced by the firm.

Koch, Robert, *Louis C. Tiffany-Rebel In Glass*, Crown Publishers, New York, 1964. A pioneering volume tracing the history and development of the Tiffany Studios from its early days to its decline.

Kraus/Sikes Inc., *Contemporary Crafts For The Home*, Kraus/Sikes Inc., New York, 1990. Domestic applications of contemporary crafts, including lamps by the author.

McKean, Hugh F., *The Lost Treasures Of Louis Comfort Tiffany*, Doubleday & Co., New York, 1980. An evaluation of Tiffany's works by a student of the original Tiffany Foundation of Laurelton Hall, Tiffany's Long Island estate.

Neustadt, Egon, *The Lamps Of Tiffany*, The Neustadt Museum Of Tiffany Art, Inc, New York, 1970. The bible of Tiffany lamps. Includes detailed descriptions of lamps and bases for collectors and artists.

Reytiens, Patrick, *The Technique Of Stained Glass*, Watson-Guptill, New York, 1973. A technical handbook on stained glass techniques and processes. An all-encompassing guide to the basics of the stained glass craft.

Sowers, Robert, *The Language Of Stained Glass*, Timber Press, Oregon, 1981. The most insightful and intelligently written treatise on the unique aesthetics of stained glass to date.

Uecker, Wolf, *Art Nouveau and Art Deco Lamps and Candlesticks*, Abbeville Press, New York, 1986. A worldwide survey of turn-of-the-century and early 20th century glass and lampmakers. Includes information on Tiffany and many other period lampmaking firms.

Untracht, Oppi, *Metal Techniques For Craftsmen*, Doubleday & Co., New York, 1975. An exhaustive, illustrated guide to decorative metal techniques and processes. Includes valuable information on metal finishing and patina.

TITLES ON SAFETY

The following books and periodicals are recommended for those developing a quality library for their health and safety program and for Right To Know training materials.

BOOKS AND PAMPHLETS

American Conference of Governmental Industrial Hygienists, 6500 Glenway Ave., Bldg. D-7, Cincinnati, OH 45211-4438. Phone: 513-5661-7881. Publications 1 and 2 are updated yearly.

1. **Threshold Limit Values And Biological Exposure Indices.**
2. **Industrial Ventilation: A Manual Of Recommended Practice**
3. **The Documentation Of TLVs and BEIs.**

Clark, Nancy; Cutter, Thomas; McGrane, Jean-Ann; *Ventilation-A Practical Guide*, Center For Safety In The Arts, New York, 1980. A guide to basic ventilation principles and step-by-step guidance for those who wish to evaluate, design and build an adequate ventilation system. Available from CSA, 5 Beekman St. New York, NY 10038

Hawley, Gessner, *Hawley's Condensed Chemical Dictionary, 11th edition*, revised by Sax, N. Irving and Lewis, Sr., Richard, Van Nostrand Reinhold, New York, 1987. (Also available from the ACGIH. Call 513-661-7881 for publication catalog.)

Rossol, Monona; Sloan, Julie, Ed., *The Professional Stained Glass (PSG) Safety Manual*, The Right To Know Program For Stained Glass Studios, The Edge Publishing Group, Brewster, NY, 1991.

Rossol, Monona, *The Artist's Complete Health And Safety Guide*, Allworth Press, New York, 1990. A guide to safety and OSHA compliance for those using paints, pigments, dyes, metals, solvents and other art and craft materials.

Sax, Irving N. and Lewis, Richard J., *Dangerous Properties Of Industrial Materials, 7th Edition*, Van Nostrand Reinhold Co., New York, 1988. (Also available from the American Conference Of Government Industrial Hygienists. Call (513)-661-7881 for publication catalog.)

The MSDS Pocket Dictionary, J.O. Accrocco, Ed., Genium Publishing Corp., Rev., 1988. A handy dictionary of terms used on material safety data sheets. Contact Genium Publishing at 1145 Catlyn St., Schenectady, NY 12303-1836. 518-377-8854.

GOVERNMENT PUBLICATIONS

Stained glass employers should first determine if they are regulated under state or federal OSHA rules. State regulated employers should contact their state OSHA for publications and compliance materials. Those under the federal law will find the following materials useful.

All workplaces should have a copy of the sections of **The Code Of Federal Regulations (CFR)** *that applies to their work. These are in the General Industry Standards: 29 CFR 1900-1910. Call your nearest OSHA office for information on obtaining copies.*

For extra help in complying with the Hazard Communication Standard (federal Right To Know) the following publications are available free from OSHA's Publication Office, Room N-3101, 200 Constitution Ave., N.W., Washington, DC 20210; 202-523-9667.

1. Chemical Hazard Communication, OSHA 3084, a booklet describing the rule's requirements.

2. Hazard Communication Guidelines for Compliance. A booklet to help employers comply with the rule.

Also available for $18.00 from the Superintendent Of Documents, U.S. Government Printing Office, Washington, DC 20210; (202)-783-3238:

Hazard Communication: A Compliance Kit, OSHA 3104, GPO order no. 929-022-00000-9, a step-by-step guide to compliance.

This page intentionally left blank

Index

Notes

Notes

Notes

Notes

Notes